SOCIAL SKILLS FOR TEENS MADE EASY

STEP-BY-STEP GUIDE TO IMPROVE
COMMUNICATION, MAKE FRIENDS, MANAGE
SOCIAL ANXIETY, AND BUILD CONFIDENCE IN 30
DAYS, EVEN IF YOU ARE SELF-CONSCIOUS

SYDNEY PARKER

Copyright © 2024 by Sydney Parker

All rights reserved.

No part of this book may be reproduced in any form or by any electronic or mechanical means, including information storage and retrieval systems, without written permission from the author, except for the use of brief quotations in a book review.

INTRODUCTION

Have you ever felt like you're on the outside looking in? Maybe you've been at a party, clutching a solo cup and wishing you knew just what to say, or perhaps you've sat through a group project feeling like you're the only one who just can't jump into the conversation. If any of this sounds familiar, you're not alone.

Once, during my own high school years, I found myself sweating bullets at a school dance, unable to muster the courage to talk to anyone. It wasn't until a kind soul, seeing my distress, reached out with a simple "Hey, it's louder here than a concert, right?" that I realized all it took was a moment, a phrase, to break the ice. That night wasn't just about survival; it was a stepping stone in my journey toward mastering the world of social interaction.

Indeed, I've been right where you are. My own journey through the maze of communication has given me a wealth of understanding to share. This book represents the best of what I've learned, driven by my desire to guide you through the complex social landscape. I've played every part—the quiet one on the sidelines, the one leading the conversation, and everything in between, from battling nerves to embracing confidence. I'm here to share the insights I've gathered with you.

"Social Skills for Teens Made Easy: Step-by-Step Guide to Improve Communication, Make Friends, Manage Social Anxiety, and Build Confidence in 30 Days, Even if You Are Self-Conscious" is designed with you in mind. Over the next 30 days, you will embark on a transformative journey. Each day, you'll be met with a reflective journal prompt, engaging activities, or a fun and tailored quiz to help you grow. We'll cover everything from the basics of making small talk to the finer points of digital etiquette.

This book isn't just a guide; it's a conversation—a conversation that understands the laughs and struggles of being a teenager. Whether you're dealing with a racing heart at the thought of speaking up in class or just looking for ways to expand your circle of friends, this book has something for you. I've included stories from well-known personalities who, just like you, faced their own social challenges and came out stronger on the other side.

As we dive into the various sections, each themed to tackle different aspects of social skills—from understanding your emotions to stepping up as a leader—you'll find this book is your ally. It's written to guide you through the sometimes overwhelming landscape of social interactions, providing clear, actionable steps and celebrating every little victory along the way.

So, whether you consider yourself shy or just socially curious, I invite you to turn the page and take the first step. Let's unlock your potential together, one day at a time. Ready to start? Why not turn that social anxiety into social prowess and transform those awkward moments into stories you'll one day share as triumphs? Welcome to a journey of becoming the best version of yourself.

SECTION 1: BUILDING A FOUNDATION OF SELF-CONFIDENCE

"I've had my doubts. I've had a lot of moments when I didn't feel confident enough to take a role, and I didn't know if I could do it."

EMMA WATSON, ACTRESS AND
ACTIVIST

Have you been in a situation where it felt like you're the only one who didn't get the memo? Like, maybe everyone else attended a secret workshop titled "How to Be Smooth and Effortlessly Cool 101"? You're not alone in feeling this way, and guess what? The secret to breaking through this invisible barrier isn't found in having a fire haircut or knowing the right people. It starts inside your head, with what you tell yourself daily.

The not-so-secret sauce to growing your social prowess is self-confidence; a big chunk of that comes from your conversations with yourself. Yes, I'm talking about the voice in your head that either pumps you up or drags you down. In this section, we're going to turn down the volume on that inner critic and tune into a channel that's more like your own personal hype station. Ready to flip the switch? Let's crank up the confidence with some positive self-talk vibes.

DAY 1: THE POWER OF POSITIVE SELF-TALK: REWIRING THOUGHTS

First, let's shine a light on that sneaky culprit known as negative self-talk. It's like a background app on your phone that slowly drains your battery; you might not even notice it's there, but it's sapping your power all the same. Phrases like "I can't do this" or "I'm not good enough" are classic hits on the negative self-talk chart-toppers. But where do these thoughts come from? Often, they're the echoes of past criticisms or failures, and our brain keeps replaying them, trying to protect us from future flops.

Now, how do you switch tracks from these downer tunes to something more upbeat? Here are some DJ tricks for your brain: affirmation exercises and thought substitution. Affirmations are like your personal cheerleading squad chanting positive statements about your abilities and worth. Start with something simple like, "I am capable of more than I realize," and say it with conviction, preferably in front of a mirror. Thought substitution means catching those negative thoughts in the act and swapping them out with a positive or realistic one. Think of it as switching from a sad playlist to a hype playlist.

Let's put this into practice. Suppose someone criticizes your project in class. Instead of spiraling into "I'm terrible at this," pause and flip the script. Remind yourself, "I can learn from this feedback," or "Everyone has off days." By regularly practicing these swaps, you'll find that positive thoughts start to come more naturally, like getting better at a video game the more you play.

Consistently choosing positive thoughts can transform more than just your momentary mood. Research shows that a positive outlook can lead to better stress management, enhanced problem-solving, and improved relationships—all essential for successful social interactions. Think of it as upgrading your mental software to run more efficiently in social settings, making you not just a participant in conversations but a confident contributor.

Armed with these tools, you're well on your way to silencing those nagging doubts and amplifying the thoughts that elevate you. Remember, the goal here isn't to never have a negative thought again—that's nearly impossible. Instead, it's about recognizing those thoughts for what they are: just thoughts, not facts. With practice, you'll start to notice a shift not only in how you think but in how you act and interact. Who knows? Maybe at the next school dance, you'll offer a shy peer a comforting word, turning their evening around just like someone did for mine. Keep tuning into your new mental playlist, and let the good vibes roll!

Journal Entry Prompt

How did it feel to identify and challenge your negative thoughts today? Reflect on a specific moment when a negative thought arose. What did you tell yourself to counter it? Did you notice any immediate changes in your emotions or physical sensations? How did this shift impact the rest of your day, interactions, or decisions? Consider whether you found it easier or harder to stay positive as the day progressed.

_____

_____

DAY 2: UNDERSTANDING YOUR SELF-WORTH: BEYOND THE MIRROR

Let's talk about mirrors—not just the ones you use to check your hair or practice those TikTok dance moves. I mean the metaphorical mirrors that reflect how we see ourselves. Often, what we see doesn't just come from us. It's a collage of opinions, expectations, and the glossy, filtered snapshots of people's lives we scroll through daily. But here's the kicker: understanding your self-worth is like realizing that you're the artist, not just the canvas. You get to decide which influences to brush onto your self-image and which ones don't make the cut.

First up, let's do a little inventory of your awesomeness. Yes, you've got strengths and achievements worth celebrating, even if they might not all be trophy-and-ribbon material. Maybe you're the friend everyone knows will keep their secrets, or perhaps you have a knack for making people laugh when they need it most. These qualities are gold. So, grab a pen and paper, or open a new note on your phone, and start listing things you're good at and moments you've felt proud of yourself. Big or small, write them all. This isn't just feel-good fluff; it's about recognizing the unique mix of traits and successes that make you, well, you.

Now, let's tackle those sneaky negative perceptions. We've all got them, and they often stem from comparing ourselves to others—thanks, social media. Say you see someone acing a test or getting tons of likes on a post, and suddenly you feel like you're not measuring up. Here's a technique to try: reframe your thinking. Instead of "I'm not as smart as them," how about "Everyone has their strengths, and I'm working on mine"? Or swap "I'll never be that popular" with "I value genuine connections, and I'm loved by my friends." This isn't about putting on rose-colored glasses; it's about adjusting your focus to give yourself a fair shot.

Choosing role models thoughtfully can also boost your sense of self-worth. Pick out people who reflect the kind of authenticity and values you admire, not just those with the most followers or fame. These might be athletes who've overcome adversity, artists who defy norms, or leaders who stand up for what's right. Think about how their journeys resonate with your own values and aspirations. What qualities do they have that you see in yourself or want to develop? Let their stories remind you that everyone has struggles and that overcoming them is part of what can make you great.

Lastly, let's get real about the filters—not the Instagram kind, but the cultural and social filters that shape how we see ourselves and others. Our world is loud with messages telling us how to look, act, and feel. It's a lot. But here's a thought: what if you could curate these influences as carefully as you curate your social media feed? Start by noticing which messages make you feel good about yourself and which make you doubt your worth. Lean into the books, shows, music, podcasts, and even friend groups that lift you up and reflect the diverse, beautiful reality of the world—not a photoshopped version of perfection.

You're taking control of your self-worth by actively choosing how you see yourself and what influences you let in. It's not always easy, but it's definitely worth it. So next time you catch your reflection—in a mirror, a window, or the eyes of someone who cares about you—remember that you're seeing a work in progress, a masterpiece that's all your own. Keep painting, refining, and stepping back to admire how far you've come.

Quiz: Understanding Your Self-Worth

1. What are metaphorical mirrors?

    a) Physical mirrors used to check your fabulous hair
    b) Opinions and expectations that reflect how we see ourselves
    c) Social media selfies

2. Why is it important to recognize your personal strengths?

    a) To compare them with others, like a competition
    b) To celebrate and build a positive self-image like a boss
    c) To win shiny trophies and ribbons

3. What should you do when you notice negative self-talk?

    a) Ignore it like background noise
    b) Accept it as accurate because why not
    c) Challenge it and replace it with a positive thought,
    like a mental ninja

4. Which of the following is an example of a positive affirmation?

    a) "I'm not as cool as others"
    b) "Everyone has their strengths, and I'm working on
    mine"
    c) "I'll never be that popular, so why try?"

5. How can choosing role models thoughtfully impact your self-worth?

    a) It can make you feel like a potato
    b) It can inspire you to develop qualities you admire
    and become a superhero
    c) It has no impact on self-worth because who cares

6. What should you do about cultural and social messages that make you doubt your worth?

    a) Ignore all messages and become a hermit
    b) Curate influences that make you feel good about
    yourself, like a personal DJ
    c) Accept all messages as gospel truth

7. True or False: Understanding your self-worth means never having negative thoughts again.

a) True, you'll be like a positivity robot

b) False, because even superheroes have off days

Answer Key:

1. b) Opinions and expectations that reflect how we see ourselves
2. b) To celebrate and build a positive self-image like a boss
3. c) Challenge it and replace it with a positive thought, like a mental ninja
4. b) "Everyone has their strengths, and I'm working on mine"
5. b) It can inspire you to develop qualities you admire and become a superhero
6. b) Curate influences that make you feel good about yourself, like a personal DJ
7. b) False, because even superheroes have off days

～

DAY 3: SETTING ACHIEVABLE GOALS: SMALL STEPS TO BIG CHANGES

Imagine playing a video game where the final boss seems light years away, and you're just armed with a beginner's toolkit. It seems daunting, right? Well, setting life goals can sometimes feel just as intimidating, especially when the endgame is something as big as "Become the most charismatic person at school" or "Ace all my courses this semester." But fear not! Just like in video games, there's a strategy to leveling up in real life, too. It's called setting SMART goals. SMART stands for Specific, Measurable, Achievable, Relevant, and Time-bound. Each goal you set should be a clear and achievable mini-mission within a specific time frame.

Let's break it down with a common teen scenario: improving your grades in math. A SMART goal would be, "I will improve my math grade from a B to an A by the end of the semester by practicing math problems for at least 30 minutes each day." See how specific and time-bound that is? It's not just "get better at math"—which is as vague as saying "be more awesome." It's precise, giving you a clear target to hit and a way to measure your progress.

Now, let's talk about breaking down larger goals. Say you want to become more socially active. That's a marathon, not a sprint, and it's about adding layers of interactions, not diving into the deep end without a life jacket. Start small. Your first goal might be, "I will start a conversation with one new person each week for a month." Each conversation is a step towards that larger goal. Think of each small goal as a checkpoint in your favorite game. You're not just running aimlessly; you're passing these checkpoints and gaining the confidence to move on to the next level.

Consistency and patience are your best friends in this game. It's like building muscle. If you've ever tried to lift weights, you know you don't just start by bench pressing 200 pounds. You start small, stay consistent, and gradually build up your strength. The same goes for any skill, including social skills. There might be days when it feels like you are making no progress at all or like you're the awkward turtle at the party. That's okay. Every expert was once a beginner. Keep at it, keep setting small, achievable goals, and you'll find that you're building not just skills but confidence.

And here's the fun part: celebrating milestones. Let's say you've managed to talk to a new person each week for a month. That's a milestone! Celebrate it. Consider treating yourself to a movie night out or a small party with close friends. These celebrations act like save points in your journey, moments to reflect on how far you've come and recharge your batteries for the next leg of the adventure. They remind you that progress is still progress, no matter how small. And when you look back, all those small steps will add up to a giant leap towards your bigger goals.

As you set out to conquer your personal quests, remember that the path to achieving big changes is through setting small, manageable, SMART goals. Keep your objectives clear and your actions consistent, and don't forget to celebrate your victories. Each small step is a piece of the puzzle in completing the grand picture of your aspirations. And before you know it, you'll look back amazed at the distance you've covered, one SMART goal at a time.

Activity: Setting Achievable Goals. Create a SMART Goal

Identify a Goal - Think of something you want to achieve socially, like making new friends or joining a club.

Make it SMART:

— Specific: Define your goal clearly.
— Measurable: Decide how you'll track progress.
— Achievable: Ensure it's realistic.
— Relevant: Make sure it matters to you.
— Time-bound: Set a deadline.

Example - Goal: "I will start a conversation with one new person each week for the next month to build my social skills and confidence, beginning with classmates and gradually moving to new acquaintances."

Write down your SMART goal and review it regularly!

DAY 4: CONSTRUCTIVE SELF-CRITIQUE: GROWING FROM FEEDBACK

Let's face it: getting feedback can sometimes feel like swallowing a spoonful of cough syrup. It might not always taste great, but it's supposed to help you get better, right? The trick is in knowing how to tell the difference between feedback that's like that beneficial, although bitter, syrup, and the kind that's just plain bitter. Understanding this can transform potentially discouraging experiences into powerful growth moments.

Constructive criticism is like a personal trainer for your skills—it's meant to challenge and strengthen you, not tear you down. It focuses on specific actions or behaviors rather than attacking you as a person. For example, if a teacher comments, "Your essay had some interesting points, but the arguments could be clearer with more supporting evidence," that's constructive. It's clear, specific, and aimed at helping you improve. On the flip side, destructive criticism often feels like a low blow. It's vague and personal, something like, "Your essay was terrible." There's nothing to learn from here; it's just disparaging.

When you receive constructive criticism, think of it as a cheat code to level up. The first step in taking feedback gracefully is to listen—really listen—without rushing to defend yourself. It's about keeping your cool and staying open to the possibility that there's room for improvement. Let's say your soccer coach suggests you need to work on your passing skills. Instead of getting defensive, a simple

"Thanks, I'll practice that" can go a long way. Later, when you're on your own, you can process what was said. Reflect on the feedback objectively: What's the core message? How can it help me improve? This reflection turns input into a tool rather than a weapon.

Self-evaluation is like doing a reality check on yourself. It's about stepping back and looking at your performance with a clear, unbiased eye. Start by asking yourself some reflective questions: What went well in that presentation? What didn't go as planned? Why? Be honest with yourself, but also be kind. The goal here isn't to beat yourself up but to figure out your strengths and where you could use a little boost. It's also about recognizing that growth is a continuous process. Every step forward, no matter how small, is progress.

Another great technique is to set up your own 'feedback sessions' with yourself. After completing a task or reaching a milestone, take a moment to jot down what you learned, what you could have done differently, and how you can apply this knowledge in the future. This habit not only cements what you've learned but also prepares you to handle external feedback better because you've already assessed yourself.

Now, for the fun part—turning feedback into action. This is where the magic happens. Start by breaking down the feedback into actionable steps. If your debate coach says you need to work on your rebuttals, plan specific ways to improve, like watching skilled debaters in action or practicing with a teammate. Create a mini-action plan: What will you do? When will you do it? How often? By breaking it down into smaller, manageable tasks, the feedback becomes less daunting and more doable.

Remember, the goal of feedback is improvement, not perfection. It's about getting better, step by step. Each piece of advice is a stepping stone to becoming more skilled, knowledgeable, and, yes, more confident in your abilities. So, next time you receive feedback, embrace it like a secret tip-off in your favorite game. It might just be the clue that leads you to your next big win.

As you continue to navigate through your teen years, remember that feedback is not something to dread but something to welcome with open arms. It's the magic ingredient in the recipe for personal growth and success. Embrace each piece of advice, each constructive critique, as a golden opportunity to refine your skills and develop into the person you aspire to be. Keep pushing forward, keep refining, and most importantly, keep growing. Your future self will thank you for it.

Activity: Constructive Self-Critique

Learn to distinguish constructive criticism from destructive criticism and use feedback for personal growth.

Identify feedback - Think of a recent piece of feedback you received. Write it down.

Analyze the Feedback - Determine if the feedback was constructive or destructive.

— Constructive feedback example: "Your presentation was good, but you could improve by speaking more slowly."

— Destructive feedback example: "Your presentation was terrible."

Reflect and Plan - Reflect on the constructive feedback. Ask yourself, "What can I learn from this?"

Create a mini-action plan to improve based on
the feedback. For example, "I will practice
speaking slowly in front of a mirror for 10
minutes each day."

By distinguishing and reflecting on feedback, you can turn it
into a powerful tool for personal growth.

~

CELEBRATING SMALL VICTORIES: KEEPING A VICTORY JOURNAL

Imagine every small win celebrated like a championship
victory—crowd roaring, confetti flying. That's the essence
of a victory journal. It's your personal space to acknowledge
and celebrate daily achievements, making you the MVP of
your own life. A victory journal is simply a record of your
successes, big or small, from mastering a challenging subject
to forming a new friendship. It serves as a tangible
reminder of your capabilities, acting as your personal
cheerleader and boosting your confidence whenever doubts
arise.

Effective journaling captures your experiences and feelings
in any form that resonates with you—be it bullet points,
sketches, or stickers. Focus on the details. For instance,
rather than merely noting, "Talked to a new classmate," delve
into how you felt before, during, and after the conversation.
Did you experience a surge of joy? Documenting these
nuances helps you appreciate your achievements when revisiting your entries. Consistency matters. Although daily
entries aren't mandatory, establishing a routine like a weekly
check-in can maintain your momentum. Think of this as

your opportunity to celebrate the week's accomplishments and reflect on your growth.

Everything that makes you proud qualifies as a victory. Whether it's participating in class, initiating a conversation, or maintaining positivity through tough times, each achievement is a step forward in your personal development journey and deserves recognition. Even subtle wins, like avoiding negative interactions or adhering to your study plan, are significant markers of your resilience and growth.

A victory journal is more than a record; it's a reflective tool that highlights your evolving confidence and skills. Regular reviews can reveal progress and patterns, such as increased ease in social situations or the formation of new friendships. This process not only celebrates your journey but also aids in setting future goals. Recognizing past successes can boost your confidence to take on new challenges, from joining clubs to leading projects. Incorporating victory journaling into your routine underscores your continuous achievements and development. It transforms your journey into a celebration of progress, encouraging you to acknowledge and build upon your successes.

Activity

Secure a notebook or journal for your entries. If cost is a concern, opt for a free digital app or repurpose any available notebook. This will be your space for reflection and goal setting.

*From the smallest seed, a resilient tree begins its journey,
rooting itself firmly in the earth. Like self-confidence, it starts
small but holds the promise of growth and strength, nourished
by the belief in one's potential.*

SECTION 2: OVERCOMING SOCIAL ANXIETY

"I think my nerves come from a place of feeling like I want to give it my all. But as I've gotten older, I've realized that everyone feels that way, and you just have to push through it."

EMMA STONE, ACTRESS

Walking into a room and suddenly feeling like your brain has turned into that annoying buggering icon on a slow internet day? Your heart's racing, your palms are sweaty, and you're pretty sure if someone spoke to you, you'd accidentally spit out your last Google search instead of a greeting. Welcome to the wild world of social anxiety. It's like your brain's natural fight or flight response is a superhero that thinks every social interaction is a villain. But don't worry, even superheroes have their off days, and this section is all about turning your social anxiety from a super-nuisance into your superpower.

UNDERSTANDING SOCIAL ANXIETY: THE WHAT AND WHY

According to Merriam-Webster, social anxiety is "a form of anxiety that occurs in social situations where one fears being judged or scrutinized by others." This feeling of nervousness or fear can make everyday interactions feel overwhelming for many teens. It's like feeling butterflies in your stomach, but a lot more intense. But remember, it's something many people experience, and there are ways to manage it and feel more confident.

Social anxiety often stems from embarrassing or stressful past experiences. It's amplified by pressures from social media and the high academic expectations placed on teens today. These factors can make social situations feel overwhelming.

This condition can follow you beyond school, affecting your willingness to engage in social activities and impacting your academic performance and relationships. It's like being a spectator in your own life, present but not fully participating.

Contrary to some beliefs, social anxiety is common among teens and possible to overcome. It doesn't mean changing who you are; instead, it means learning to feel more comfortable in your own skin. Knowing what social anxiety is, its triggers, and how it affects you is the first step toward regaining control. It's about learning to navigate through your anxiety, not waiting for it to disappear. Let's prepare to lower the volume of your anxiety and amplify your life instead.

Harness the overlooked superpower of your breath to counteract social anxiety. Diaphragmatic or belly breathing is a simple yet effective method to induce calmness, shifting from panic to peace by activating your body's relaxation response.

Quick Guide to Belly Breathing

- Find a Quiet Space: Sit or lie down in a comfortable position.
- Position Your Hands: One on your chest, the other on your belly.
- Inhale Slowly: Through your nose, allowing your belly to rise more than your chest. Count to four.
- Exhale Gradually: Through your mouth for six counts, focusing on the hand on your belly to ensure proper diaphragm engagement.
- Tools: Visual aids and apps can enhance your practice.

Utilize belly breathing before social situations or whenever anxiety creeps in. It's a subtle, powerful technique to armor yourself against stress. It's beneficial both as an immediate calm-provider and a long-term resilience builder.

Incorporating this practice daily can remarkably reduce anxiety, boost concentration, improve sleep quality, and elevate your overall well-being. It equips you with the confidence to navigate social interactions, helping to transform anxiety into manageable serenity.

DAY 5: BUILDING A SUPPORT SYSTEM: FINDING YOUR ALLIES

Imagine trying to play a team sport all by yourself. Sounds pretty harsh, right? That's a bit like what dealing with social anxiety can feel like when you're going solo. Having a solid support system is like having the ultimate backup team; it's necessary when tackling the big plays or even just the daily grind. This network isn't just about having people to hang out with—it's about building a team that can pass you the ball when you're blocked, cheer you on when you make that game-winning shot, and help you strategize when you're up against formidable opponents in the form of anxiety.

Now, identifying these allies might feel a bit like scouting for talent. You need people who understand the game you're playing—those who get what it's like to feel anxious in social settings or are empathetic enough to support you even if they don't fully understand the experience. These allies could be friends who notice when you're feeling overwhelmed and can step in with a distraction or a quick escape route. Family members who give you space when you need it but are there to listen when you're ready to talk are invaluable. Even teachers or counselors who recognize your struggle and can provide professional guidance or just a safe space to breathe can be part of this support squad.

So, how do you put this team together? Start by opening up about what you're dealing with. It might be tempting to keep your feelings under wraps, but letting people in is like sending out a signal flare. You'd be surprised how many people are ready and willing to stand by you once they understand what you're facing. Reach out to those you trust and try expressing what kind of support you need, whether it's someone to talk to when you're feeling anxious, someone who can accompany you to social events, or just someone who understands your need for occasional solitude. It's like instructing your teammates on the best plays that can help you win; "Hey, I feel really anxious in large groups. Could we hang out somewhere quieter?" or "I get nervous talking in class. Could you help me practice?"

Building this support system is staying ahead of the game, not just playing catch-up. Why not create a buddy system or a small group among your peers who share similar experiences with anxiety? This can be your go-to group for discussing what's working (or not), sharing strategies, and just having each other's backs. It's about creating a community where everyone speaks the same language of understanding and support, a mutual fan club where everyone is rooting for each other. This isn't just about leaning on others; it's about building mutual support where you are all allies for each other, sharing the load and lifting each other up.

This kind of network doesn't just buffer against the impacts of social anxiety; it actively enhances your overall mental wellness. Each interaction within a supportive group can reinforce the feeling that you are not alone, that others share your experiences or at least understand them, and that support is always at hand. It's about transforming your social anxiety from a solo struggle into a team effort, where every player has a vital role in supporting each other. So, start scouting for your team, reach out for support, build those connections, and strengthen your mutual support systems. With the right people around you, social anxiety can become just another opponent you know how to outplay together.

Journal Prompt: Building Your Support System

Reflect on the people in your life who make you feel understood and supported. Who are your current allies, and how have they helped you manage social anxiety or difficult situations? Write about one person who has been particularly supportive and describe a specific instance where their support made a difference. Then, think about areas where you might need more support and brainstorm ways to build

or strengthen your support system. How can you reach out
and communicate your needs to others?

_____

_____

_____

_____

_____

~~~⌇~~~

DAY 6: MINDFULNESS IN ACTION: STAYING PRESENT IN SOCIAL SITUATIONS

Do you sometimes find yourself zoning out in the middle of
a conversation or worrying about all the ways you could
potentially embarrass yourself at the next school event?
That's your brain, the drama queen, taking you on a need-
less anxiety trip. Here's where mindfulness, your chill
cousin, steps in. Mindfulness is all about living in the now,
not in the "what ifs" or the reruns of past embarrassments.
It's like having a mental remote control that helps you
switch off the unnecessary drama and tune into what's
happening right in front of you. By focusing on the present,
you give less power to your anxiety and more power to
yourself in managing how you feel and react in social
settings.

Mindfulness isn't just some fancy buzzword; it's a practical tool. For instance, say you're at a party and start feeling overwhelmed by the noise and the number of people. A quick mindfulness exercise could be focusing entirely on a conversation with a person next to you. Listen to their words, notice their expressions, and engage actively. This focused attention helps anchor you in the moment, pushing out anxiety and making the social interaction more manageable and enjoyable. Another simple practice is the "5-4-3-2-1" technique, where you quickly ground yourself by naming five things you can see, four you can touch, three you can hear, two you can smell, and one you can taste. It's like hitting the reset button on your nervous system, pulling your mind away from anxiety triggers and back to reality.

Integrating mindfulness into your daily routine can start small. Maybe begin by spending a few minutes each morning doing nothing but listening to the sounds around you. Or, try mindful walking on your way to school, where you focus entirely on the experience of walking, feeling your feet hit the ground, noticing your breath, and observing what's around you without judgment. Making mindfulness a regular practice can help lower your baseline level of anxiety, making those spike moments of panic less intense. It's like training your mind to be a calm, cool observer of your own life, giving you the power to enjoy each moment more fully.

Let's look at some real-life examples. Consider Jamie, a teen who always felt like an outsider in social situations, worried about saying the wrong thing or not fitting in. By practicing mindfulness, Jamie learned to focus on the flow of interactions rather than over-analyzing every word. This shift allowed for more natural conversations and, surprisingly, more invitations to hang out.

Then there's Morgan, who used mindfulness to manage performance anxiety during school presentations. By focusing on the present moment, Morgan could concentrate on the message rather than the fear of audience judgment, leading to more confident and compelling presentations.

These stories underscore that mindfulness isn't about being perfect or never feeling anxious; it's about managing life's stresses in real time, giving you the tools to stay present and connected, even when anxiety tries to hijack the moment. Whether you're dealing with daily social interactions or specific anxiety-inducing events, mindfulness offers a way to navigate through them with greater ease and confidence. So next time you feel overwhelmed, remember that mindfulness is just a breath away. Practice it, embrace it, and watch how it transforms your experiences, one moment at a time.

Quiz: Answer the following questions to see how well you can wield the power of mindfulness like a social superhero.

1. What is mindfulness?

   a) Reliving your most embarrassing moments on repeat
   b) Staying in the present, like a Zen master
   c) Stressing over next week's math test

2. How can mindfulness help you at a party?

   a) By turning you into a social ninja, fully engaged and present
   b) By letting you teleport home
   c) By making you the loudest person in the room

3. Which mindfulness technique is like a superhero's sensory scan?

  a) "5-4-3-2-1" technique
  b) "Counting sheep" (Zzzz...)
  c) "Mindful moonwalking"

4. What's your mission during a mindfulness exercise at a noisy party?

  a) Tune into the noise and start a solo dance party
  b) Worry about saying something silly
  c) Become a conversation superhero by focusing entirely on the person next to you

5. How can you sneak mindfulness into your daily routine?

  a) Walk to school like you're in a zombie apocalypse
  b) Crank up your tunes and block out the world
  c) Play detective: Listen to morning sounds and soak in your surroundings

6. How did Jamie level up social interactions with mindfulness?

  a) Overanalyzed every word like a mad scientist
  b) Focused on the flow of interactions like a social surfer
  c) Avoided social scenes like a ninja in hiding

Answer Key:

  1. b) Staying in the present, like a Zen master

2. a) By turning you into a social ninja, fully engaged and present
3. a) "5-4-3-2-1" technique
4. c) Become a conversation superhero by focusing entirely on the person next to you
5. c) Play detective: Listen to morning sounds and soak in your surroundings
6. b) Focused on the flow of interactions like a social surfer

~

DAY 7: ROLE-PLAYING SCENARIOS: PRACTICING SOCIAL INTERACTIONS

Imagine you're gearing up for a big game—let's say, the championship of socializing. Just like in sports, you wouldn't jump into the final match without a bit of practice and a game plan, right? That's where role-playing swoops in. It's like your personal social skills gym, where you can flex those interaction muscles in a no-risk environment. Think of it as a rehearsal for real-life social events, where slipping up is part of the process and not a social catastrophe.

Role-playing is a fantastic method to experiment with different social interactions because it lets you navigate various scenarios in a controlled, safe setting. It's a space where mistakes are not only allowed but are expected—it's all part of the learning curve. You can try out different ways to start a conversation, handle a tricky social situation, or even learn how to exit a chat without that awkward "umm, I gotta go water my cat" excuse. The beauty of role-playing is that it builds your confidence. The more you practice, the less scary real-life interactions become. You start to realize that social slip-ups aren't the end of the world—they're just stepping stones to becoming more able to navigate the social sphere.

Let's dive into crafting these scenarios. Start with situations that are common but might stir up a bit of anxiety. Picture walking into a party where you only know the host or tackling a group project where you need to collaborate with classmates you've never spoken to before. How about the classic: making new friends during lunch? By setting the stage for these interactions, you can script out potential dialogues and responses. For instance, what are some ways to break the ice? How might you ask someone about their interests without coming off as too intense? Role-playing allows you to explore these questions in a low-pressure environment, tweaking your approach as you go.

Feedback is a golden nugget in role-playing. It's like having a coach who points out what moves are scoring points and where you might need to tweak your strategy. This feedback should be constructive and focused on specific behaviors, not just a pat on the back or a vague "that was weird." For example, if your voice tends to get really high when you're nervous, your role-play partner can point that out, and you can work on keeping your tone more relaxed. Or maybe you tend to talk over people when you get excited. Feedback will help you recognize these habits so you can consciously keep them in check.

Starting with more straightforward interactions is the key. You wouldn't lift the heaviest weights on your first day at the gym, and the same goes for social role-playing. Begin with scenarios that feel slightly uncomfortable but doable. As your confidence muscles grow stronger, you can gradually increase the complexity of the interactions. Maybe start with asking a classmate about a homework assignment and work your way up to debating a topic in front of the class. Each step up takes you further out of your comfort zone and deeper into becoming a social pro.

Through role-playing, you're not just learning about how to handle specific situations; you're also learning about yourself —your strengths, your nervous ticks, and how you react under social pressure. This self-awareness is a critical component of personal growth. It will serve you well beyond high school halls and college campuses. So, step into the role-play arena, try on different social hats, and discover the best ways to express yourself. Each scenario is a scene in the great play of your social life, and you're the star—it's time to act like it!

Activity: Role-Playing Scenarios - Tackling a Group Project

Gather a Partner - Find a friend or family member to role-play with you.

Set the Scene - Imagine you're in a classroom, and you've been assigned to a group project with classmates you don't know well.

Role-Play - Scenario 1: Introducing Yourself

— You: "Hi everyone, I'm [Your Name]. I'm excited to work on this project with you all. What do you think about starting with brainstorming ideas?"

Scenario 2: Discussing Roles

— You: "I have some ideas for the project outline. Does anyone have a preference for specific tasks? I can handle the research part if that works for everyone."

Give feedback - After each scenario, your

partner gives constructive feedback on your
introduction and collaboration approach.
Focus on specifics like tone of voice, clarity,
and engagement.

Reflect - Write down one thing you learned and
one thing you want to work on.

Example: "I felt more confident introducing
myself. Next time, I'll try to ask more open-
ended questions to involve everyone."

As we wrap up this section on overcoming social anxiety, remember that the strategies discussed here are tools in your toolkit. From understanding what social anxiety really is, building a supportive network, and mastering calming techniques like deep breathing and mindfulness to practicing through role-playing—each strategy offers a unique way to manage and eventually minimize the impact of anxiety in your social life.

Armed with these tools, you're better equipped to face the social challenges ahead with confidence and poise. As we transition into the next section, we'll explore how to further enhance these skills, ensuring that you're not just surviving social interactions but genuinely thriving in them.

As the tree sprouts its first leaves, it begins to stretch towards the sky, breaking through the confines of its shell. Overcoming social anxiety is much like this, a gradual but steady reaching out toward the light of connection and understanding.

SECTION 3: MASTERING COMMUNICATION SKILLS

"Just be yourself, there is no one better."

TAYLOR SWIFT

Picture this: You're at a bustling party, or maybe it's just lunchtime in the cafeteria. You spot someone you've wanted to chat with for ages. They're sipping on their drink or maybe picking at their food, and there's a golden window of opportunity. What do you do? If your plan so far has been to blend into the wallpaper and hope they notice your awesome shirt, let's just put that plan on hold. It's time to level up your convo skills, and this section is like your personal trainer for communication muscles you didn't even know you had.

Starting conversations and keeping them flowing aren't just skills for late-night talk show hosts or politicians; they're essential tools for, well, everyone! Whether you're trying to make new friends, impress your crush, or simply get through a family dinner without awkward silence, you need to master the art of conversation. So, buckle up! We're about to dive into the nuts and bolts of chatting like a champ.

~

DAY 8: ART OF CONVERSATION: STARTING ENGAGING DIALOGUES

Let's kick things off with how actually to start a conversation. Initiating dialogue can be as nerve-wracking as a squirrel on its first espresso, but it doesn't have to be. The secret? Open-ended questions. These are the kinds of questions that require more than a yes or no answer. They're your golden ticket to a flowing conversation. For instance, instead of asking, "Did you like the movie?" (to which they can reply simply "yes" or "no"), try "What did you think about the movie?" This version invites them to share more, and just like that, you're off to the races.

Using current topics or events as conversation starters is another smooth move. It could be as simple as, "Hey, did you catch the game last night?" or "What did you think of that science presentation today?" It's about finding common ground quickly and hitching your wagon there. Remember, the goal is to get the conversation rolling. You're the spark; what follows could be a delightful dialogue fire!

Now that you've started, let's keep the ball rolling. The objective here is to show genuine interest. People love talking about their interests and experiences, and showing that you care about what they're saying not only keeps the conversation going but also makes it more enjoyable. Follow-up questions are your best friends here. If they mention they play guitar, follow up with, "How did you get started with that?"

or "What's your favorite song to play?" Each question opens up a new branch in the conversation tree, and before you know it, you're swinging from topic to topic like a pro.

Sharing related stories or experiences is another way to deepen the conversation. It's like a lively chat over coffee; they share a story, and you respond with one of your own. This back-and-forth keeps the conversation balanced and engaging. Just make sure not to hijack the dialogue; it's about sharing the stage, not performing a solo!

Ah, the dreaded awkward silence. It sometimes sneaks up like a ninja right in the middle of a chat. Don't panic! Use it as a moment to regroup. One way to break the silence is by changing the subject. It's like hitting the refresh button. You could jump to a new topic with something like, "Speaking of movies, have you seen any good ones recently?" Or even use the pause to compliment them: "By the way, I really like your jacket. Where did you get it?" Just like that, you're back in the game.

All good things must come to an end, including conversations. Exiting a chat gracefully is just as necessary as starting one. You want to leave on a high note, making sure the other person feels good about the interaction. Summarize a part of the conversation to show you were paying attention: "I loved hearing about your trip to Spain; it sounds like it was an amazing experience!" Then, part with some polite and positive words, like "It was great chatting with you! Let's catch up again soon." This not only ends the conversation smoothly but also sets the stage for future interactions.

Mastering the art of conversation is like learning to dance. At first, you might step on a few toes or feel a bit clumsy. Still, with practice, you'll be twirling through dialogues at social gatherings, school events, or even in everyday chats.

It's about being present, being genuine, and, most importantly, being yourself. With these tools in your communication toolkit, you're ready to turn every conversation into an opportunity to connect, impress, and express yourself. So go ahead and step into your next social interaction with confidence—the floor is yours!

Journal Prompt: The Art of Conversation

Reflect on a recent conversation in which you struggled to keep the dialogue going or felt nervous starting it. Using the tips from this section, how could you have initiated the conversation differently? What open-ended questions might you have asked to keep the conversation flowing? Also, think about a time when you handled an awkward silence or exited a conversation gracefully. Write about what you did and how it made you feel. How can you apply these strategies to future conversations to make you feel more confident and engaged?

_____

_____

_____

_____

DAY 9: LISTENING SKILLS: HEARING BEYOND WORDS

So, you've nailed starting a conversation and keeping it bouncing back and forth like a good game of ping pong, but how about your listening game? Is it as sharp as your chatting skills? Listening sounds simple—just stay quiet and let the other person do the talking, right? But authentic listening, the kind that builds strong connections, is more like decoding a secret message rather than just nodding along. It's about actively engaging with what the other person is saying and showing that you really get them. Let's unpack some killer listening techniques that can turn you into the listener everyone wants to chat with.

Active listening is all about showing that you're fully tuned in and deeply engaged. It's not just about hearing words; it's about connecting. Start with your body language: nod occasionally to show you're following along, make eye contact, and maintain a posture that says, "I'm all ears!" It's like your body says, "Go on, I'm with you." Now, reflect back on what's being said. This doesn't mean you echo every word, but a quick, "So, you felt really excited when you achieved that?" shows that you're not only listening but also processing their words. This kind of feedback can make all the difference in how valued and understood someone feels during a conversation.

Now, onto the traps we all fall into sometimes. Top of the list? Interrupting. Sure, it's tempting to jump in with your own story or an opinion, but cutting someone off mid-sentence can make them feel like you're more interested in hearing your own voice than theirs. Another pitfall is preparing your response while the other person is still talking. It's like your brain is so busy drafting the next presidential speech that it forgets to listen. This can lead to missing key details, making the conversation feel disjointed. And let's not forget the big one: showing disinterest. Whether it's glancing at your phone or looking over your shoulder, these actions shout, "I'm not really interested in what you're saying," louder than words.

Listening isn't just about what is said; it's also about catching what isn't said—the pauses, the sighs, the shift in tone. These non-verbal cues can tell you heaps about what the other person is really feeling. For instance, pausing after mentioning a test might suggest they're anxious about it, even if they're playing it cool. A quick change in pitch might reveal excitement or irritation that they're not openly expressing. Tuning into these subtleties can give you deeper insight into the person's emotions and thoughts, allowing you to respond more empathetically and appropriately.

Lastly, let's talk about sealing the deal in active listening. Providing feedback that confirms understanding can significantly enhance the quality of your interactions. Summarize or paraphrase parts of the conversation to show you've been paying attention, like, "So, you're saying that you felt overlooked during the meeting?" This not only shows you're engaged but also allows the other person to clarify if you've misunderstood anything. Asking follow-up questions also plays a role here. Questions like, "What happened next?" or "How did that make you feel?" show that you're interested in digging deeper and understanding the whole picture.

By stepping up your listening game with these techniques, you're not just being polite but opening doors to deeper relationships and more meaningful connections. Whether it's with friends, family, or even teachers, showing that you genuinely listen can make you the person everyone wants to talk to. So, next time you're in a chat, put these skills to the test. Dive into the art of listening, not just to respond but to understand and connect on a whole new level.

Quiz: Listening Skills - Hearing Beyond Words

1. What is the primary goal of active listening?

    a) Nodding like a bobblehead
    b) Connecting deeply and showing understanding
    c) Preparing your next joke while they talk

2. Which of these is a sign of active listening?

    a) Staring off into space
    b) Nodding, maintaining eye contact, and reflecting back what's said
    c) Constantly checking your phone

3. What should you avoid doing to be a good listener?

    a) Interrupting with your own stories
    b) Smiling and nodding
    c) Asking follow-up questions

4. How can you show that you're interested in what the other person is saying?

    a) Glancing around the room
    b) Reflecting back their words and asking follow-up questions
    c) Saying "uh-huh" repeatedly without really paying attention

5. Which of these actions can make someone feel like you're not interested in their words?

a) Leaning in and nodding
b) Glancing at your phone or looking over your shoulder
c) Maintaining eye contact and summarizing their points

6. What's a good way to handle a pause or a sigh during a conversation?

a) Ignore it and keep talking
b) Ask if there's something on their mind or how they're feeling
c) Change the subject immediately

7. Why is reading between the lines in a conversation important?

a) To pass time until it's your turn to talk
b) To understand the speaker's emotions and respond empathetically
c) To impress them with your mind-reading skills

Answer Key:

1. b) Connecting deeply and showing understanding
2. b) Nodding, maintaining eye contact, and reflecting back on what's said
3. a) Interrupting with your own stories
4. b) Reflecting back their words and asking follow-up questions
5. b) Glancing at your phone or looking over your shoulder
6. b) Ask if there's something on their mind or how they're feeling

7. b) To understand the speaker's emotions and respond empathetically

⌇

DAY 10: BODY LANGUAGE BASICS: WHAT YOU SAY WITHOUT SPEAKING

Do you know the feeling of walking into a room and feeling like someone was upset, even though they hadn't said a word? Or maybe you've seen someone try to hide their excitement, but their wide eyes and quick movements gave it all away. That's the power of body language—it speaks volumes without making a sound. Whether you realize it or not, the way you sit, stand, smile, or frown can communicate just as much as any words that come out of your mouth. Mastering the art of body language can dramatically transform your ability to communicate effectively. So, let's break down what your body could be telling other people and how you can make sure it's saying what you actually mean.

First off, non-verbal cues include all the ways you communicate without words. This encompasses facial expressions, gestures, posture, and even how much space you take up. For instance, think about what a furrowed brow and crossed arms suggest compared to a smile and open hands. The first combo screams, "Back off!" while the second one is practically an invitation to chat. Being aware of these cues in yourself and others can help you read a room better and adapt your behavior to better fit the situation. It's like having a secret insight into what everyone is really thinking, which can be super helpful in navigating social interactions, from tense group projects to chill hangouts.

Now, onto crafting the right signals. Positive body language, like smiling and an open posture, can make you seem approachable and friendly. Smiling not only makes you more attractive but also emits enthusiasm, making others feel more comfortable around you. An open posture—like not crossing your arms or legs—suggests you're open to communication and willing to engage. Mirroring, or subtly copying someone else's body language, is another powerful tool. If they lean in, you lean in; if they lower their voice, you do the same. This can create a feeling of empathy and understanding, showing that you are engaged and in tune with how they are feeling.

On the flip side, certain types of body language can throw up barriers. Crossed arms can make you appear defensive or closed off, even if you're just cold or trying to get comfortable. Avoiding eye contact might make you seem disinterested or, worse, like you have something to hide. And let's not forget fidgeting, which can signal nervousness or impatience. While it's totally normal to feel anxious or restless, unchecked fidgeting can be distracting and might make others feel uneasy. Being conscious of these signals and adjusting your body language can help prevent miscommunications and make your interactions smoother and more positive.

Finally, it's imperative to align your verbal and non-verbal cues. Have you ever told someone you were fine when you were clearly upset? Your words said one thing, but your body likely told the truth. When your body language doesn't match your words, it can confuse the listener and make you seem untrustworthy or insincere. Striving for consistency between what you say and how you say it helps reinforce your message and builds trust with others. If you're excited about something, let your whole body show it. If you're apologizing, make sure your posture and expressions convey sincerity. This alignment not only helps others understand you better but also boosts your confidence in your communication skills.

By becoming more aware of your body language and the signals you're sending, you can take your communication skills to a whole new level. It's not just about using your words wisely; it's about making your entire body talk the talk. Whether you're aiming to make new friends, ace a job interview, or just get through a family dinner, paying attention to the unspoken dialogue can make all the difference. So, next time you find yourself in a social setting, take a moment to assess not just what you're saying but how you're saying it—all without saying a word.

Quiz: Body Language Basics - What You Say Without Speaking

1. What is body language?

    a) The way you dance like nobody's watching
    b) Non-verbal cues like facial expressions, gestures, and posture
    c) Using interpretive dance to communicate

2. What do a furrowed brow and crossed arms typically suggest?

    a) You're trying to become a human pretzel
    b) Defensiveness or frustration
    c) You're just really cold and need a hug

3. Which of the following is an example of positive body language?

a) Smiling and having an open posture

b) Pretending to be a statue

c) Tapping your foot like you're in a drum solo

4. How can mirroring someone's body language help in a conversation?

a) It makes you look like a synchronized swimmer

b) It creates a sense of empathy and understanding

c) It confuses the other person into thinking you're their twin

5. What should you avoid doing to prevent sending negative body language signals?

a) Crossing your arms and turning into a human pretzel

b) Maintaining eye contact like you're in a staring contest

c.) Nodding so much you look like a bobblehead

6. Why is it essential to align your verbal and non-verbal cues?

a) To create a secret dance language

b) To make you seem like a mind reader

c) To reinforce your message and build trust

Answer Key:

1. b) Non-verbal cues like facial expressions, gestures, and posture
2. b) Defensiveness or frustration
3. a) Smiling and having an open posture

4. b) It creates a sense of empathy and understanding
5. a) Crossing your arms and turning into a human pretzel
6. c) To reinforce your message and build trust

DAY 11: ASSERTIVENESS TRAINING: EXPRESS YOURSELF WITHOUT FEAR

Let's talk about assertiveness, not to be confused with its distant cousins, aggression and passivity. Imagine assertiveness as the Goldilocks of communication styles—it's just right. It's about being upfront about your needs and feelings without stepping on anyone else's toes. This isn't about transforming you into a debate champ who dominates every conversation, nor is it about making you a wallflower who only nods and smiles. Assertiveness is about finding that sweet spot where your voice is heard just as loudly as everyone else's.

So, what exactly is assertiveness? It's the ability to express your thoughts, feelings, and beliefs in an open, honest, and direct way while still respecting others. It's not about being pushy (that's aggression) or mumbling your opinion and hoping someone hears (that's passiveness). Assertiveness is your communication backbone; it lets you stand up for yourself without knocking others down. This skill is crucial not just in dodging peer pressure or handling a disagreement but also in everyday interactions, like choosing a movie with friends or discussing a poor grade with a teacher. It's about being respectful yet firm, clear yet courteous.

Now, how do you actually communicate assertively? Enter "I" statements, a game-changer in the world of communication. Instead of saying, "You make me so mad," which sounds pretty confrontational and might put the other person in defensive mode, try, "I feel upset when you interrupt me because I think what I have to say matters too." See the twist? This approach focuses on your feelings and perceptions without blaming or accusing the other person. It's like saying, "Here's what's up with me," without adding, "...and it's all your fault." Using "I" statements helps keep the conversation calm and focused and opens the door for productive, respectful dialogue.

Conflicts are like vegetables—nobody's favorite part of the meal but inevitable and good for you if handled right. Assertiveness shines brightest in these tricky situations. It's about expressing your viewpoint clearly and respectfully while also being open to hearing the other side. Say you're in a group project, and two members have conflicting ideas. Instead of picking sides or avoiding the tension, you could steer the conversation with, "I see both points have their merits. How about we find a compromise that incorporates both ideas?" This approach not only diffuses tension but also shows that you value both perspectives. It's about navigating the conflict, not escalating it.

Journal Prompt: Assertiveness Training: Express Yourself without Fear

Reflect on a recent situation where you felt you weren't able to express your thoughts or feelings openly. How did it make you feel, and what was the outcome? Using the techniques discussed in this section, think about how you could have approached the situation more assertively. Write down an "I" statement you could have used to express yourself clearly and respectfully. For example, "I feel frustrated when our gatherings run late because it affects my ability to complete other tasks." How do you think using assertiveness might have changed the outcome?

_____

_____

_____

_____

_____

DAY 12: THE POWER OF EMPATHY: CONNECTING ON A DEEPER LEVEL

Imagine you're watching one of those movies where the main character feels what everyone else is feeling. Sounds exhausting, right? But also, imagine how understanding they are in their relationships. That's empathy in a nutshell—not so much feeling everyone's emotional baggage but understanding and sharing their feelings as if they were your own. Empathy is like a super glue for human connections; it's what helps us bond and understand each other on a deeper level. And when it comes to talking and listening, empathy turns ordinary exchanges into meaningful conversations.

So, what exactly is empathy? It's the ability to put yourself in someone else's shoes—to understand their feelings and perspectives without judgment. It's seeing the world through their eyes and connecting with their emotions. Why is this important? Because empathy breeds compassion and trust, the foundations of any strong relationship. Whether it's with friends, family, or even acquaintances, empathy allows you to navigate social interactions more smoothly, making others feel valued and understood. It's a crucial skill in building bridges and healing wounds, not just in personal relationships but also in broader social contexts.

Empathetic listening is about more than just hearing words; it's about tuning into the emotions behind them. Imagine a friend telling you about a rough day at school. Instead of just nodding and thinking about what to say next, empathetic listening involves really hearing their frustration and disappointment. You might reflect this understanding back to them by saying, "That sounds really tough. It must have been frustrating to deal with that." This kind of response not only shows that you are listening but that you also care about their feelings. Techniques like mirroring their emotions or summarizing what they've said are great ways to practice empathetic listening. It's about making the speaker feel seen and understood, which can significantly deepen the connection between you.

But empathy isn't just about listening; it's also about how you respond. Expressing empathy can transform a simple conversation into a bridge of deeper understanding. It involves more than just understanding someone's emotions —it's about validating them and showing genuine concern. For instance, if someone is excited about a new project, express your excitement with them. Say something like, "That sounds amazing! You must be thrilled!" This kind of empathetic response not only acknowledges their feelings but also shares in their emotional experience, creating a shared moment of joy.

Empathy really shows its strength in sensitive or difficult situations. For example, suppose you're in a heated debate. In that case, trying to see the other person's point of view can help de-escalate the situation. It allows you to address conflicts with a cooler head and a warmer heart. Even in everyday interactions, empathy can smooth over potential bumps. It helps you understand where the other person is coming from, which can prevent misunderstandings and build a more supportive environment. Whether you're consoling a friend who's going through a tough time or trying to understand a parent's perspective on curfews, empathy can open doors to more effective and compassionate communication.

By weaving empathy into your conversations, you're not just talking; you're connecting on a human level. This doesn't mean you have to agree with everyone all the time or take on everyone's emotional baggage. It's about acknowledging their feelings as valid and trying to understand their perspective. This can lead to more meaningful relationships and a greater sense of connection with those around you. As you continue to practice empathy, you'll find that it not only enriches your conversations but also enriches your relationships, making them stronger and more resilient.

Activity: Empathy in Action

Develop your empathetic skills through observation and reflection.

> Observation Journal: Spend a day observing the interactions around you. Pay close attention to the body language, facial expressions, and

tones of voice of people you encounter.
Note down specific instances where you
think someone is expressing a strong
emotion, like happiness, frustration, or
sadness.

Reflect on Feelings: In your journal, write a
short reflection for each instance you
observed. Try to describe what the person
might be feeling and why. For example, "I
noticed my friend seemed quiet and withdrawn during lunch. They might be feeling
overwhelmed or sad because they have a lot
of schoolwork."

Empathy Mapping: Choose one of the
instances you observed and create an
empathy map. Divide a piece of paper into
four sections labeled "Says," "Thinks," "Does,"
and "Feels." Fill in each section with what
you think the person was expressing
verbally ("Says"), what they might be
thinking ("Thinks"), their actions ("Does"),
and their emotions ("Feels").

Action Plan: Think about how you could
respond empathetically in one of the situations you observed. Write down a few
sentences of what you might say to show
empathy. For example, "If I notice my friend
is quiet and seems sad, I might say, 'You
seem a bit down today. Do you want to talk
about what's bothering you?'"

Practice Empathetic Responses: Over the next
few days, try to apply your action plan in
real interactions. Observe the responses you
get and how they change the dynamics of

your conversations. Note any positive
changes or challenges you encounter.

Example Observation and Reflection:

Observation: I saw my classmate, Charlie,
    looking stressed before our math test. He
    was pacing and frowning.
Reflection: Charlie might be feeling anxious
    about the test because he mentioned he
    didn't have much time to study.
Empathy Map:
— Says: "I didn't get much time to study."
— Thinks: "I'm worried I won't do well."
— Does: Pacing, frowning.
— Feels: Anxious, stressed.
Action Plan: "Hey Charlie, I noticed you seem a
    bit stressed about the test. Do you want to
    go over some main points together before it
    starts?"

As we wrap up this section on mastering communication
skills, remember that each skill—whether it's starting
conversations, listening actively, understanding body
language, asserting yourself, or practicing empathy—plays a
vital role in enhancing your ability to connect with others.
These skills go beyond mere communication tools; they
serve as pathways to a richer understanding and more
fulfilling connections. Continue to refine these abilities, and
you'll see a remarkable transformation in your social interactions, making each conversation a step toward stronger and
more meaningful relationships. Up next, we'll dive into navigating digital social spaces, where communication takes on
new challenges and opportunities in the digital age.

*With each new branch, the tree extends its reach, much like
mastering communication. It learns to spread its influence and
connect with others, creating a network that supports its
continued growth and vitality.*

SECTION 4 NAVIGATING DIGITAL SOCIAL SPACES

"Be yourself; everyone else is already taken"

OSCAR WILDE

I magine your online persona as a digital superhero version of you. Now, what if I told you that sometimes, without even noticing, we might be creating a persona that's a bit too over-the-top or polishing an image that's just a little too perfect? Navigating the social media universe requires more than just flashy posts; it's about crafting an online identity that indeed echoes who you are, not just who you think you should be. Let's dive into the art of staying authentic online, dodging the pitfalls of a fabricated image, and keeping it real across different platforms.

∾

DAY 13: MANAGING YOUR ONLINE PERSONA: STAYING TRUE ONLINE

Creating and maintaining an online persona that genuinely reflects your true self and values isn't just about avoiding a few fibs about your weekend activities. It's about aligning your digital expressions with your real-world self. Think about the aspects of your personality you're proud of—maybe it's your quirky sense of humor, your passion for art, or your advocacy for mental health. These are the gems to highlight in your online persona. But here's the kicker: authenticity. It's the secret ingredient that makes your digital self resonate with others. When you share real experiences, genuine thoughts, and true feelings, you create deeper connections than any filter could ever manufacture. So next time you post, ask yourself, "Is this me, or is it just what I think looks cool?"

Now, let's talk about the flip side: the risks of rocking a more fake than a true persona. Crafting an image that's far removed from who you really are can lead to a host of troubles, like the classic case of trust issues. Suppose your friends or followers discover the disconnect between your online persona and your actual life. In that case, their trust can evaporate faster than a Snap story. Beyond that, maintaining a false front is like wearing a mask that's too tight—it's uncomfortable, and you can't keep it on forever without slipping. Plus, the stress of upholding a fabricated image can really weigh you down. Why choose that when being your genuine self is so much lighter?

Keeping your online persona consistent across different platforms is like making sure your story stays the same whether you're on Instagram, TikTok, or Snapchat. It doesn't mean you can't tailor your content to fit the vibe of each platform

—go ahead and get artsy on Insta and goofy on TikTok—but the core, the real you, should remain unchanged. Consistency helps you build a coherent brand for yourself, one that's easily recognizable and reliably genuine. It's about making sure that whether someone scrolls through your TikTok dances or your Insta stories, they're getting the same authentic slice of your life.

Let's bring in some real-life flavor. Consider Jamie, who once juggled multiple online personas—one for each social media platform. Instagram Jamie was an adventurer climbing mountains every weekend (even though he actually just climbed the stairs to his apartment), while on Twitter, Jamie was a hot-take artist on all things political (despite not being able to vote yet). It was exhausting and confusing. Eventually, Jamie decided to simplify his digital life, aligning his online presence with his real interests—comic books and coding. The result? He had deeper connections with followers who shared his genuine passions and a lot less stress about keeping up false pretenses.

Or take Peyton, who initially hid her love for anime on social media because she thought it was "too nerdy." When she finally started sharing her artwork inspired by her favorite shows, she was overwhelmed by the positive response. She discovered a community of fans just like her. This authenticity brought her not only closer friendships but also opportunities to collaborate with other artists and creators. By embracing her true self, Peyton turned her social media into a portal of opportunities and genuine interactions.

Navigating your digital social spaces with authenticity and consistency isn't just about crafting a likable online persona; it's about creating a space where you can connect truthfully and freely. It's about letting your digital footprint be a true reflection of your footsteps in the real world. So, next time you log in, remember that the best character you can play online is yourself.

Quiz: Managing Your Online Persona - Staying True Online

1. What's the secret ingredient to making your digital self resonate with others?

    a) Posting only pictures of your pet rock
    b) Authenticity
    c) Pretending to be a time-traveling wizard

2. What can happen if your online persona is more fake than true?

    a) Your friends will think you're a secret superhero
    b) You might face trust issues and feel like a stressed-out pineapple
    c) You'll gain the ability to speak fluent dolphin

3. How can you keep your online persona consistent across different platforms?

    a) By posting cat memes exclusively
    b) By staying true to your core self while tailoring content to fit each platform's vibe
    c) By using the same filter that makes you look like a space alien

4. What lesson did Jamie learn from juggling multiple online personas?

a) It's fun to have different personas everywhere, like being a secret agent

b) Simplifying his digital life and being genuine led to deeper connections and less stress

c) It's easy to confuse everyone and make them think you're a shape-shifter

5. How did Peyton benefit from sharing her true interests online?

a) She discovered she's actually a wizard in disguise

b) She found a community of fans, made closer friendships, and got new opportunities

c) She had to join a secret society of anime enthusiasts

Answer Key:

1. b) Authenticity
2. b) You might face trust issues and feel like a stressed-out pineapple
3. b) By staying true to your core self while tailoring content to fit each platform's vibe
4. b) Simplifying his digital life and being genuine led to deeper connections and less stress
5. b) She found a community of fans, made closer friendships, and got new opportunities

DAY 14: CYBERBULLYING: DEALING WITH DIGITAL HARASSMENT

Let's tackle a challenging but essential topic—cyberbullying. Imagine you're just chilling, scrolling through your feed, and then, bam, you find nasty comments or direct messages aimed at tearing you down. Not cool, right? Cyberbullying is like the villain of the digital world, lurking behind screens and sowing negativity. It's more than just a disagreement or a one-off rude comment; it's a repeated pattern meant to intimidate, embarrass, or insult. Think of texts, posts, tweets, or memes that keep targeting someone to make them feel small or scared. This digital menace can sneak up in many forms, whether it's spreading rumors, sharing embarrassing photos without consent, or hurling insults. Understanding what qualifies as cyberbullying is the first step in fighting back.

Now, how do you deal with these digital bullies? First up, know when to pick your battles. If it's just a random mean comment, sometimes the best response is no response. Ignoring the bait can often make trolls lose interest. But what if it doesn't stop? Or what if the comments are seriously harmful? That's when you step up your game. Respond, but keep it classy and calm. A simple "Please stop; your comments are hurtful" might do the trick. However, if the harassment escalates, it's time to bring in reinforcements—report the behavior to the platform and talk to someone you trust, like a parent or teacher. They can help you take further action, like contacting the cyberbully's parents or even the authorities if things get really serious.

Preventing cyberbullying starts with guarding your digital gates. Tighten up your privacy settings so only people you trust can see your posts or send you messages. Think of it as setting up a sound security system in your digital house. Also, be mindful of who you connect with online. Not everyone who sends a friend request or follows you need to be let into your virtual space. It's okay to be selective; after all, your online wellbeing is at stake.

Support is paramount when dealing with cyberbullying. Remember, you're not alone in this. Websites like StopBullying.gov provide resources and advice on handling cyberbullying effectively. Many social media platforms have guidelines and tools for reporting abusive content and behavior, making it easier to take action against bullies. Schools often have policies and counselors who can offer support and intervene if necessary. Knowing these resources can empower you to stand up against cyberbullies with confidence.

Navigating the digital world can sometimes feel like walking through a minefield, but understanding the ins and outs of cyberbullying, knowing how to respond, and taking preventive measures can make you a savvy and safe digital citizen. Equip yourself with knowledge, and don't hesitate to seek help when needed. Your online space should be a place of positivity and self-expression, not fear or negativity. So, keep these tips in your back pocket and surf the web boldly and wisely.

Journal Prompt: Cyberbullying: Dealing with Digital Harassment

Reflect on a time when you or someone you know experienced negative behavior online. How did it make you feel, and what steps did you take to address it? If you could go back, what would you do differently using the tips mentioned in this section? Write about how you can strengthen your online privacy and support systems to protect yourself and others from cyberbullying better. How can you contribute to creating a more positive and supportive digital community?

_____

_____

_____

_____

_____

~~~≫⊱⊰≪~~~

DAY 15: SOCIAL MEDIA BALANCE: ONLINE AND OFFLINE LIFE

Let's face it: the digital world has its perks, but sometimes, it feels like we're all starring in a movie where smartphones are glued to our hands—plot twist, it's actually reality! While scrolling through feeds and snapping pics can be loads of fun, it's vital to catch the signs when social media starts playing the villain in your real life. Maybe you've noticed that your legs feel as stiff as a pair of jeans left out in the cold because your daily walks have turned into scrolling marathons. Or perhaps real conversations have become as rare as an unfiltered selfie, and your sleep schedule is as erratic as a cat in a laser pointer factory. These are the flashing neon signs that social media might be steering your life a bit off course.

Recognizing these red flags is the first step. The next is setting boundaries—because managing your social media isn't about cutting it out of your life; it's about ensuring it doesn't overshadow everything else. Think about creating specific hours for when you dive into the digital world. Maybe decide that meal times are phone-free or that after 9 p.m., your phone gets as much sleep as you do. Establishing tech-free zones or periods can also work wonders. Perhaps make your bedroom a sanctuary where phones fear to tread or keep the dinner table a place for face-to-face chats instead of digital distractions. It's about creating pockets of peace where real life gets the spotlight, not just the screen glare.

Now, let's chat about the unsung heroes of your story—offline activities. Remember the simple joys of shooting hoops, diving into the pages of a gripping novel, or hiking through nature? These activities aren't just fun; they're like personal trainers for your wellbeing. Engaging in sports can boost your physical health and teach teamwork while losing yourself in a book enhances empathy and reduces stress. And let's not forget the magic of being in nature; it's like hitting the refresh button on your soul. Each of these activities offers a unique blend of benefits that help you grow stronger, smarter, and more connected to the world around you. They remind you that a big, beautiful offline world is waiting to be explored—a world where experiences are felt, not just filtered.

Balancing online and offline life is truly an art form in today's digital age. It's about weaving through your day with the awareness to know when to log in and when to log off. Imagine managing your time like a DJ mixes tracks. Sometimes, you're tuned into the digital beat; other times, you're grooving to the live vibes of the world around you. It's about finding that rhythm that keeps your social life enriched and varied, ensuring that your digital interactions are just part of a larger, vibrant social dance. So, as you navigate this connected world, keep tuning into the cues of your own needs and make sure that your tech habits don't drown out the beautiful complexities of face-to-face connections and real-world adventures. Keep the balance, and you'll not only enhance your social skills but enrich your life with a diversity of experiences that no online platform can replicate.

Activity: Balancing Online and Offline Life

Self-Assessment - Spend a day noting how much time you spend on social media and other online activities. Use a journal or a time-tracking app to record your usage.

Identify Red Flags - Reflect on your notes and identify any red flags such as feeling stiff from sitting too long, missing out on in-person interactions, or disrupted sleep patterns.

Set Boundaries - Choose at least two boundaries to implement. Here are some examples:

— Designate tech-free times (for example, no phone use after 9 p.m. or during meals).

— Create tech-free zones (for example, no phones in the bedroom or at the dinner table).

Explore Offline Activities - Make a list of three offline activities you enjoy or would like to try. Examples include playing a sport, reading a book, going for a hike, or practicing a hobby like drawing or playing an instrument. Schedule time for these activities in your weekly agenda or task tracker.

Tech-Free Challenge - Choose one day in the next week to take the "Tech-Free Challenge."

Commit to spending at least half the day without any social media or unnecessary online activity. Use this time to engage in the offline activities you listed.

Reflection - At the end of the week, reflect on your experience. Write about how the tech-free time made you feel. Did you notice any changes in your mood, focus, or relationships? Were there any challenges? How can you continue to balance your online and offline life moving forward?

Example Schedule:

Social Media Challenge

7-Day Challenge

Monday - Track social media usage. Identify red flags.

Tuesday - Set boundaries (e.g., no phone use during dinner). List offline activities.

Wednesday - schedule offline activities.

Thursday - Begin implementing tech-free times.

Friday - Continue implementing tech-free times.

Saturday - Tech-Free Challenge Day.

Sunday - Reflect on the week and plan for ongoing balance.

DAY 16: DIGITAL ETIQUETTE: RULES OF ONLINE ENGAGEMENT

Navigating the digital world is a lot like attending a giant, never-ending party. Everyone's invited, and while it's buzzing with exciting conversations, it's also a place where manners matter. That's where digital etiquette comes into play—it's the rulebook for behaving properly online. Think of it as the unwritten code that helps keep interactions respectful and constructive. Understanding digital etiquette starts with some basics: think before you post, respect others' opinions, and be mindful of the impact your words and images can have. It's easy to forget that behind every profile picture and username is a real person with real feelings. So, before hitting that post or comment button, take a moment to consider how your words could affect them.

One of the biggest social mistakes in the digital world is oversharing. Sure, it's tempting to share every detail of your life online, from your breakfast burrito to your late-night thoughts about the universe. But remember, the internet never forgets. Oversharing can not only bore your audience but also expose you to risks like identity theft or just plain embarrassment. Another common mistake is posting sensitive content without thinking. Whether it's a heated opinion post or a photo from that wild party last weekend, ask yourself if it's something you'd be comfortable with everyone seeing—from your best friend to your grandma to a future employer.

Engaging in online arguments can also be a slippery slope. The anonymity of the internet can lead some to say things they would never say face-to-face, turning what could be a healthy debate into an all-out war. If you find yourself in a heated discussion, take a deep breath and strive for a polite and respectful tone. Remember, winning an argument isn't worth losing a friend or sullying your online reputation.

Now, let's talk about how to keep your digital interactions positive. Using polite language goes a long way. Simple phrases like "please" and "thank you" can soften requests and show gratitude, making others more receptive to your messages. Being inclusive is also important. The internet is a global village, full of diverse cultures, viewpoints, and backgrounds. Embracing this diversity not only enriches your online experience but also promotes a sense of community and respect.

Disagreeing respectfully is perhaps one of the most valuable skills in digital etiquette. It's perfectly fine to have different opinions, but the way you express these differences can either bridge gaps or widen them. Instead of attacking someone's viewpoint, try to understand where they're coming from and explain your perspective in a way that's open and low-key. A little compassion can turn a potential conflict into an opportunity for mutual understanding.

To bring these points to life, consider the scenario of responding to a provocative message. Imagine someone posts a comment on your video that you find offensive. Your first impulse might be to fire back with something equally harsh, but that only adds fuel to the fire. A more effective approach would be to either ignore the comment, if it's openly trolling, or respond calmly, clarifying why you find the comment inappropriate and inviting the person to a more constructive conversation. This not only maintains your dignity but also sets a positive tone for others who might read the exchange.

In another scenario, if you see someone being harassed online, stepping in can be tricky but essential. A supportive comment showing solidarity with the person being targeted can discourage the harasser and empower the victim. You might also privately message the person being harassed to offer your support and encourage them to report the harassment if it continues.

Navigating the digital landscape with proper etiquette isn't just about avoiding missteps; it's about actively creating a positive, respectful online environment. By thinking before you post, respecting diverse opinions, and engaging constructively, you help set the tone for your digital circles. Just like in real life, a little courtesy goes a long way online. Whether you're commenting on a friend's post, debating in a forum, or sharing your latest photos, how you conduct yourself can make all the difference. So, the next time you log on, remember that your words and actions contribute to the vibe of the vast digital party. Make it a good one!

Journal Prompt: Digital Etiquette: Rules of Online Engagement

Reflect on a recent online interaction. Did you handle it well, or could you have responded better? Consider these questions:

- What was the situation, and how did you respond?
- Did you follow digital etiquette rules like thinking before posting, using polite language, or respecting opinions?
- How did your actions affect the other person and the conversation?
- What will you do differently next time to ensure a positive interaction?

Write a brief plan for incorporating good digital etiquette into your daily online activities.

_____

_____

_____

_____

_____

KEEPING CONVERSATIONS POSITIVE AND PRODUCTIVE

In the digital realm, similar to a video game, you'll have fun moments and make dope connections. Still, you'll also have to deal with things like avoiding negativity and how you handle your online interactions, from DMs to comments, which shape not just your online rep but also how you interact with people in real life. Let's level up your digital communication skills to keep things respectful, avoid drama, handle disagreements smoothly, and stay positive.

Digital communication etiquette mirrors the courtesy we apply in real life, and it has changed for the online world. It's about being clear, respectful, and kind. Before sending a message, consider if you would say it face-to-face. This reflection encourages kindness and transparency, reducing the chance of misunderstanding. In digital spaces where tone can be unclear, choose words that foster positive interactions, steering clear of sarcasm and slang that could confuse your global audience.

The absence of non-verbal cues online makes it easy for messages to be misunderstood. To prevent this, provide context for your jokes or sarcasm with a simple "lol" or emoji and elaborate on more serious topics to ensure clarity. If misunderstandings occur, address them swiftly with a clarification to prevent things from getting out of hand. Clear communication minimizes confusion and maintains smooth digital interactions.

Online disagreements can get heated fast without the benefit of face-to-face interaction. When things start to get tense, take a moment to pause and think before you reply. Focus on what's being said, not who's saying it, and try to use facts and logic instead of getting aggressive. If the argument isn't going anywhere, stepping back and agreeing to disagree is okay. That way, you can keep the conversation chill and productive.

Aim to be a force of positivity in your online communities. Share uplifting content, engage positively in discussions, and offer support. Small acts of kindness, like complimenting a post or sharing helpful resources, can have a significant impact, enabling a supportive digital environment. By making it a priority to provide clear, respectful communication, you'll not only improve your online interactions but also contribute to a healthier digital community. Your next post or comment could spark a new friendship, hobby, or even future opportunity. Practice strong digital manners to improve your online world.

PRIVACY PROTECTIONS: SAFEGUARDING YOUR DIGITAL FOOTPRINT

Your digital footprint—comprising tweets, shares, and online activities—follows you everywhere in the digital realm. Unlike a shadow, it can cause trouble if not managed wisely. Online privacy means having control over your personal information, such as your name, birthday, and browsing habits. Each time you engage online by signing up for apps, posting on social media, or visiting websites, your information is collected, which could lead to identity theft or unwanted attention if mishandled. Knowing what information you're sharing and with whom matters.

Think of online privacy as a defense strategy. Begin by familiarizing yourself with the privacy settings on social media platforms like Instagram, Facebook, and TikTok, adjusting them to control who sees and interacts with your posts. Be mindful about sharing location details and personal information like your home address or school name. Limiting this sharing can protect you from potential risks.

Privacy breaches can have serious consequences, ranging from identity theft to cyberstalking, impacting both your digital and real-life well-being. Such incidents can lead to unauthorized charges on credit cards or unwelcome personal attacks, highlighting the importance of active privacy management.

Regularly reviewing your privacy settings, much like checking game stats or homework, can prevent privacy mishaps. Apps and platforms update their policies frequently, so stay informed to protect your digital presence effectively. Treat these check-ups as essential upkeep for your online health. Navigating online privacy can be challenging, but with the proper knowledge and actions, you can maintain a clean digital footprint and safeguard your personal information. As you engage online, remember to manage your digital interactions with the same care and respect as those in real life, ensuring a respectful and protected digital existence. Moving forward, we'll explore personal growth and self-discovery, emphasizing the development of your identity and values in both the online and offline worlds.

As the tree blossoms, its flowers represent the blooming of connections in digital spaces. Each flower, a new opportunity, symbolizes the diverse and vibrant interactions that help the tree—and the individual—flourish in an ever-connected world.

SECTION 5 EMBRACING INDIVIDUALITY AND AUTHENTICITY

"Why fit in when you were born to stand out?"

DR. SEUSS

D o you know what it's like when you're on an endless quest, like a character in an epic video game, trying to unlock the secret level where you finally figure out what you're genuinely passionate about? Well, spoiler alert: discovering what makes you tick isn't about stumbling upon a hidden treasure. It's more like crafting your own map as you go, marking spots of joy and intrigue. This section is your DIY kit for crafting that map and exploring territories of interest that make you, well, you! So, let's roll up our sleeves and dig into the exciting world of passions and how they weave into the fabric of your well-being.

～

DAY 17: DISCOVERING YOUR PASSIONS: EXPLORING WHAT MAKES YOU TICK

First off, let's deal with the big question: "How do I figure out what I'm passionate about?" Think about the last time you completely lost track of time doing something. Maybe you were sketching, coding a new app, or experimenting with recipes in the kitchen—activities where the world seemed to fade away, and it was just you and your craft. These are clues.

To start this exploration, grab a journal or open a new digital doc and list activities that absorb you completely. Don't judge or censor your interests; just jot them down. This list is your personal interest inventory, the raw materials we'll use to map out your passion project.

Now, with your list in hand, it's time to play mad scientist with your interests. Experimentation is vital to transforming vague interests into full-blown passions. Choose one interest from your list and dive deeper. Sign up for a workshop, join a club, or set up a personal project related to it. The goal here isn't to immediately excel but to explore. You might discover a hidden talent or realize that something isn't quite as exciting as you thought—and that's totally fine. Each experiment brings you closer to understanding what truly fires you up. Remember, Edison didn't invent the lightbulb on his first try; it took lots of attempts and learning from each failure. Approach each new activity with curiosity and resilience. Who knows? Your next try might light up your world.

While we're on this exploratory trail, let's talk about why following your passions isn't just fun but also essential for your mental and emotional health. Engaging in activities that you love can dramatically boost your mood and self-esteem. It gives you a sense of purpose and accomplishment, like adding a rare achievement badge to your life's gaming profile. For instance, consider the story of Alex, a teen who discovered a passion for photography. Through his lens, he found a new way to connect with the world, capturing moments that often went unnoticed. His anxiety, which frequently made school a challenge, found a quiet space among the clicks of his camera. This isn't just about filling time; it's about enriching your life's portfolio with experiences that resonate with your soul.

Finally, let's ensure these newfound or deepening interests don't just end up as weekend hobbies. Integrating your passions into daily life can enhance your everyday happiness and self-discovery journey. Start small; maybe it's reading a page of a novel each night, sketching during lunch, or coding for thirty minutes in the morning. Think of these activities not as additional tasks on your to-do list but as non-negotiable appointments with joy. They are as important as your daily meals—a nourishment for your spirit.

As you map out your passions and experiment with new activities, remember that this process is uniquely yours. It's about finding what makes your heart race a bit faster, your mind engage a bit deeper, and your smile stretches a bit wider. Whether it's playing guitar, coding, painting, or something entirely out of the box, each step towards recognizing and welcoming your passions is a step towards a more vibrant, authentically happy you. So keep exploring, keep experimenting, and let your passions lead you to new heights of joy and fulfillment.

Activity: Discovering Your Passions - Exploring What Makes You Tick

Interest Inventory - Spend 10 minutes listing

activities that make you lose track of time. Think about moments when you felt absorbed entirely and happy.

Choose and Explore - Pick one interest from your list to explore further this week. Research ways to dive deeper into this interest, such as online tutorials, clubs, or workshops.

Experiment - Dedicate at least 1 hour this week to experimenting with your chosen interest. Keep a journal to note what you enjoyed, what you learned, and any challenges you faced.

Reflect on Well-being - After your experiment, reflect on how engaging in this activity made you feel. Did it boost your mood? Did you feel a sense of accomplishment?

Daily Integration - Think of small ways to integrate this interest into your daily routine. Examples: Spend 10 minutes sketching each day or read a chapter of a book each night.

6. Share and Connect - Share your experience with a friend or family member. Discuss what you discovered and how you plan to continue exploring your passion.

～

DAY 18: VALUES AND BELIEFS: STANDING BY WHAT YOU BELIEVE IN

Imagine you're the main character in a video game, where each level tests not just your skills but your decisions based on your core beliefs. What do you stand for? What won't you stand for? These aren't just filler for your character's bio; they're the principles guiding your every move. Understanding and defining your personal values isn't just about building a moral compass—it's like programming your internal GPS to navigate life's twists and turns.

So, how do you start this quest of identifying your personal values? Think of moments that made you feel really proud or deeply satisfied. Perhaps it was a time when you stood up for a friend or completed a project that made a difference. Each of these moments is a clue to what you truly value. To get these values out of the abstract and into your daily life, try this: create a "Values Map." Grab a piece of paper, and write down stories from your life that felt significant. Next to each, note what value was at play—was it fairness, compassion, or imagination? Seeing your values spelled out helps solidify them in your mind and shows you when and how you're already living according to them.

Now, wielding your values isn't just about having them; it's about using them to steer your choices. Every decision, from how you handle a disagreement to what you post online, is a chance to align with your values. This alignment matters because it not only ensures consistency in your actions but also strengthens your sense of self. When faced with a tough choice, ask yourself: "Does this align with my values?" This question can be your north star, keeping you true to yourself even when external pressures push you towards easier or more popular paths. It's like having a secret weapon that shields you from choices that could lead you astray.

But here's the thing: everyone's values map looks different. And that's not just okay; it's necessary for a vibrant, diverse society. It is essential to learn to respect and understand where others are coming from, even if their values differ from yours. This doesn't mean you have to agree with everyone; instead, it's about acknowledging their right to their perspectives. This respect is the foundation of empathy and tolerance. It allows for healthier debates, more inclusive communities, and deeper connections. Think of it as being an ambassador in your own life, navigating through diverse value landscapes with respect and openness.

Putting your values into action can be one of the most rewarding aspects of knowing what you stand for. Whether it's through volunteering, participating in community projects, or standing up against injustices, these actions cement your values not just in your mind but in your world. Take, for example, teens who organize or participate in local clean-ups because they value environmental conservation or those who volunteer at food banks because they believe in helping those in need. Each act of service is a ripple, spreading the impact of your values across your community and beyond. Even everyday actions, like choosing to speak kindly or opting to share over competing, are ways to live out your values. These choices might seem small, but they are profound in their impact, reinforcing the type of person you choose to be every day.

As you continue to explore and define what you truly stand for, remember that your values are your anchors and guides. They are uniquely yours, and they give your actions and decisions both purpose and depth. Living in alignment with your values isn't just about making good choices; it's about making your choices suitable for you, ensuring they reflect the person you aspire to be. So keep reflecting, keep respecting, and keep acting in ways that speak true to the values you hold dear. This is how you craft a life that is not only successful but also significant.

Journal Prompt: Values and Beliefs: Standing by What You Believe In

Reflect on a moment when you felt incredibly proud or deeply satisfied. What happened, and what values were at play? Write about why this moment was significant to you and how it reflects your core beliefs.

Next, think about a recent decision you made. How did your values influence that decision? If you could go back, would you change anything to better align with your values?

Finally, consider how you can put your values into action in your daily life. List three actions or decisions you can make this week that align with your core beliefs. Reflect on how living in alignment with your values makes you feel and how it impacts those around you.

_____

_____

_____

_____

_____

DAY 19: THE ART OF BEING DIFFERENT: THRIVING AS YOURSELF

Let's face it: Being a teen can sometimes feel like you're auditioning for a role in a show where everyone expects you to fit a specific role. But here's a thought: what if you tossed the script and wrote your own? Embracing your uniqueness isn't just about standing out from the crowd; it's about being comfortable in your own skin, quirks and all. Think about all the most memorable characters in your favorite shows or books; don't their unique traits make them so special? That's the power of individuality, and guess what? You've got it too.

So, how do you start celebrating what makes you different? It begins with recognizing and appreciating the qualities that set you apart. Maybe you have an eclectic style, a quirky sense of humor, or an unusual hobby. These aren't things to hide; they're your superpowers. Embracing these traits can feel like a breath of fresh air like you're finally allowing yourself just to be you. And the cool part? Celebrating your uniqueness can inspire others to embrace their own differences. It creates a ripple effect that enriches your environment, making it a more diverse and vibrant place to be. Imagine a world where everyone felt free to be themselves without fear of judgment. By embracing and celebrating your own quirks, you're helping to create just that.

Of course, deciding to stand out can come with a side of anxiety about how others will react. Will they judge? Will they laugh? Here's where you need to fortify your self-confidence. Start by focusing on what you genuinely like about yourself. Make a list of your positive attributes, not just how you look but what you contribute to the world. Are you compassionate? Are you a problem solver? Write these down and remind yourself of them daily. When you feel good about who you are, others' opinions start to lose their edge. It's like wearing an invisible suit of armor; whatever gets thrown your way just bounces off.

Building this kind of confidence doesn't happen overnight. It's a process, sometimes a challenging one. But every step you take towards accepting yourself is a step away from the fear of judgment. Surround yourself with supportive friends who appreciate you for who you are, not who they think you should be. Their support can be a powerful buffer against negative judgments. And remember, most people are too wrapped up in their own insecurities to truly judge yours as harshly as you might imagine.

Now, let's talk about the perks of letting your true colors shine, especially when it comes to social situations. When you are authentically yourself, you attract people who genuinely get you. These relationships tend to be deeper and more fulfilling because they're based on real recognition and appreciation of each other's true selves. Plus, being genuine opens doors to opportunities that align with your natural passions and interests. Whether it's joining a club that matches your hobbies or taking on roles that suit your skills, being yourself helps you find the specific area where you can thrive.

Expressing yourself isn't just about how you interact; it's also about finding outlets that let your soul sing. Whether it's fashion, art, writing, or music, these are tools not just for self-expression but for communication. They allow you to say, "This is who I am," without even speaking. If you're into fashion, wear that vintage hat or those funky shoes with pride. If art is your thing, fill your spaces with creations that tell your story. Write blog posts, poems, or stories that let others peek into your world. Every stroke, stitch, or stanza is a declaration of your individuality.

Take, for instance, the simple act of customizing your backpack or your room. These personal touches are expressions of your identity. They tell a story about what matters to you, what you believe in, and what you love. And every time someone appreciates these expressions, it's a reminder that your unique perspective adds value to the world just as much as the more conventional ones.

So, as you navigate the sometimes turbulent waters of teen life, remember that your individuality is not just a trait to be tolerated but celebrated. It's what makes the tapestry of human experience so wonderfully complex and colorful. Embrace it, express it, and watch as it transforms not only your own view of the world but how the world views you.

Quiz: The Art of Being Different - Thriving as Yourself

1. What's the first step to celebrating your uniqueness?

    a) Hiding all your quirks in a secret vault
    b) Recognizing and appreciating what sets you apart
    c) Trying to be a clone of your favorite celebrity

2. How can you overcome the fear of judgment?

    a) Wear an actual suit of armor to school
    b) Focus on what you genuinely like about yourself
    and remind yourself of these qualities daily
    c) Only talk to your pet rock

3. What's a fun way to express your individuality?

    a) Dressing like everyone else

b) Customizing your backpack or room with personal touches

c) Pretending to be a secret agent in disguise

4. Why is it beneficial to be yourself in social settings?

a) It helps you blend into the background like a chameleon

b) It attracts people who genuinely get you and creates deeper connections

c) It makes you invisible

5. What should you do if you have a quirky sense of humor?

a) Hide it and only laugh in your head

b) Embrace it and make others laugh with you

c) Try to be as dull as possible

Answer Key:

1. b) Recognizing and appreciating what sets you apart
2. b) Focus on what you genuinely like about yourself and remind yourself of these qualities daily
3. b) Customizing your backpack or room with personal touches
4. b) It attracts people who genuinely get you and creates deeper connections
5. b) Embrace it and make others laugh with you

∽

DAY 20: HANDLING PEER PRESSURE: STAYING TRUE UNDER PRESSURE

Peer pressure—it's like that sneaky character in video games who pops up and tries to sway you off your mission path with tempting shortcuts or risky moves. You know the deal: everyone's doing it, so why shouldn't you? But here's the scoop: not all invitations to join the crowd are as harmless as they seem, and it's crucial to recognize when you're being nudged, pushed, or downright shoved away from your values or comfort zone. Peer pressure isn't always about the big stuff like drugs or skipping school. It can sneak into the everyday corners of your life, like being persuaded to mock someone to fit in or caving to wear something that's not 'you' just to get approval.

Recognizing these moments is the first step in mastering the art of staying true under pressure. Peer pressure can be as loud as a shout or as quiet as a whisper, suggesting you need to act a certain way to be liked or accepted. It can come from friends, classmates, or even people you look up to. But no matter the source, it's your job to stand guard. Start by asking yourself: "Does this feel right? Am I being nudged to betray my own compass?" Awareness is your shield; it gives you the clarity to see the situation for what it is—a test of your authenticity.

Now, let's talk about defense strategies. Imagine you're prepped for a showdown in your favorite game. You wouldn't go in without a plan, right? The same goes here. One solid tactic is having a set of rehearsed responses ready. These are your verbal armor pieces against peer pressure. If someone's pushing you to try something you're uncomfortable with, a simple, confident "No, thanks, I'm good" can be surprisingly effective. It shows you're firm in your decision without being confrontational. But what if the pressure doesn't back down? That's when you pull out the strategic retreat—remove yourself from the situation. It's not about running away from the battle; it's about choosing not to play a game where the rules are set against you.

Building self-assurance is like leveling up your character. The more confident you are in who you are and what you stand for, the less impact peer pressure will have on you. Start by declaring your strengths and values daily. It could be through affirmations, journaling, or simply setting small, daily challenges that you can achieve. Each success, no matter how small, builds your confidence. It's about reinforcing the idea that you are capable, you have worth, and you don't need to follow the crowd to validate that.

Let's get interactive and really put your skills to the test with some role-playing exercises. Picture this: you're at a party, and someone offers you a drink you know you shouldn't take. How do you respond? Practice this scenario with a friend or even in front of a mirror. Role-play different outcomes—maybe in one, you change the subject smoothly; in another, you explain why you choose to say no. This practice isn't just about preparing for peer pressure; it's about strengthening your ability to stand up for yourself. It's training in the art of staying true to your principles, even when the world seems to be pushing against them.

Handling peer pressure is an ongoing challenge, one that requires you to be alert, prepared, and confident. It's about knowing when to say yes, how to say no, and having the courage to walk your own path, even when others veer off. This isn't just about resisting negative influences; it's about actively choosing to live a life that's true to yourself, one decision at a time. So next time you feel the weight of peer expectations pushing down on you, remember: you have the tools, you know the tactics, and you absolutely have the strength to push back. Keep standing strong, keep your values in clear sight, and keep being unapologetically you.

Journal Prompt: Handling Peer Pressure - Staying True Under Pressure

Reflect on a time when you faced peer pressure. How did it make you feel, and what did you do in response? Write about whether you stayed true to your values or felt swayed by the pressure. What strategies could you use next time to handle similar situations better? How can you build your confidence to resist peer pressure in the future?

_____

_____

_____

_____

ROLE MODELS AND MENTORS: LEARNING FROM OTHERS' PATHS

Consider assembling a dream team for an epic video game battle; you'd pick characters with top-notch skills, right?

Similarly, in life, selecting role models and mentors is about choosing individuals whose achievements and qualities inspire you to grow. It's not just their success that matters, but the values they uphold and the traits they exhibit.

Think about who inspires you—perhaps a tech innovator, a sports icon, or a teacher with engaging classes. What specifically about them motivates you? Is it their creativity, strength, or kindness? Diving into the stories of those you admire offers a behind-the-scenes look at their paths, including both triumphs and setbacks. These narratives show that success is not a straight line but a journey with highs and lows, teaching resilience and adaptability.

For example, understanding how your favorite artist overcame early rejections can highlight the importance of persistence alongside talent. Engaging with mentors can elevate this learning. If you have the opportunity to connect with a mentor, cherish these interactions. Approach them with thoughtful questions that probe deeper than surface-level advice, such as inquiring about the obstacles they've faced and their strategies for overcoming them. This approach not only shows your respect for their insights but also provides you with tailored advice for your own path. Remember, feedback from a mentor is a treasure trove for personal growth, even if it's sometimes challenging to hear.

Consider also how you can embody the role of a mentor or role model for others. You don't need to wait until you're widely recognized; start now by demonstrating kindness, pursuing your passions, and standing up for your beliefs. Your actions can inspire those around you, contributing to a cycle of positive influence and inspiration.

Navigating life with role models and mentors offers guidance through your personal challenges and aspirations, linking you to the broader human experience of striving and achieving. By emulating the paths of those you admire and aspiring to inspire others, you contribute to a legacy of growth and inspiration that exceeds individual achievement. Remember, the figures you look up to were once in your shoes—they dared to dream, persist, and guide others. Now, it's your turn to follow in their footsteps and carve your own path.

As we conclude our journey through individuality and authenticity, remember that embracing your true self and values shapes a life uniquely yours. Discovering passions, living by your values, expressing uniqueness, navigating peer pressure, and learning from role models and mentors are all crucial steps. Each action paints your life's masterpiece.

Continue making bold choices and using vibrant colors. As we move to the next section, take these lessons and inspirations with you, lighting the way to personal growth and fulfillment.

Every leaf on the tree carries a unique pattern, a testament to the beauty of individuality. Embracing one's true self allows the tree to stand tall, its authenticity shining through each distinct branch and leaf.

SECTION 6: FORMING AND MAINTAINING FRIENDSHIPS

"Friendship is born at that moment when one person says to another, 'What! You too? I thought I was the only one.'"

C.S. LEWIS

I magine you're crafting the ultimate squad in your favorite multiplayer game. Who do you pick? The unstoppable warrior? The cunning strategist? Or maybe the loyal sidekick? Believe it or not, forming friendships in real life isn't much different. It's about picking the right mix of characters who'll stand by you during boss fights and cheer you on during victory dances. But instead of looking for someone who can wield a virtual sword, you're looking for those who wield kindness, support and a whole lot of laughs. So, how do you assemble your real-life dream team? Let's dive into the nitty-gritty of choosing friends who add value, not drama, to your life.

DAY 21: CHOOSING FRIENDS: QUALITIES OF GOOD FRIENDSHIPS

First things first: your core values. These are the deep-rooted beliefs that shape who you are and what matters most to you —like the code of honor for knights of old or the unwritten rules of conduct for modern-day superheroes. Maybe honesty tops your list, or perhaps it's loyalty or a sense of humor. Understanding your own core values is like having an internal guide; it helps you steer toward people who share similar principles. When you and your friends value the same fundamental ideas, your friendships have a stronger foundation built on mutual respect and understanding. It's like syncing your gameplay so everyone's working toward the same quest—winning together, supporting each other, and having a blast along the way.

Now, let's talk about traits—specifically, the traits that make for a good friend. Reliability is a big one. You want friends who are like that trusty old bike you can always count on to get you where you need to go—no unexpected breakdowns or last-minute bailouts. Kindness is another critical trait. A friend who spreads kindness is like a walking, talking, feel-good playlist, brightening up your days and supporting you when you're down. And let's not forget a supportive nature. A friend who's supportive is like your personal cheerleader, hyping you up for your achievements and cushioning your falls. These traits manifest in everyday interactions, often in small acts like showing up on time, listening with genuine interest, or sending you a meme just when you need a laugh. It's these little things that, when stacked together, form the bedrock of a solid friendship.

But it's not all high-fives and group selfies. There are red flags to watch out for—signals that a potential friend might not be the best addition to your squad. Inconsistency is one such red flag. If someone is your BFF one day and giving you the cold shoulder the next, alarm bells should ring. Disrespect is another major deal-breaker. It's a clear sign that they're not friend material if they don't respect your boundaries, feelings, or others. And beware of anyone who pressures you to conform—true friends celebrate your individuality, not stifle it. Recognizing these red flags early can save you from drama and heartache down the line. It's like spotting a glitch in your favorite game before it crashes your system—you're better off steering clear!

Finally, let's chat about the power of diversity in friendships. Just like a well-rounded team in sports or gaming, having friends from different backgrounds and perspectives can enrich your life immensely. It opens you up to new ideas, experiences, and ways of seeing the world. It's about adding various spices to your friendship stew, making it richer and more flavorful. Embracing diversity in your friendships encourages openness and inclusivity, making your social circle a vibrant tapestry woven from many different threads. Imagine the stories, the insights, the varied laughter—each friend adding their unique color to the palette of your life.

Choosing the right friends is about more than just sharing interests or hanging out. It's about finding people who uplift you, challenge you, and support you as you grow. It's about surrounding yourself with positivity, respect, and joy. So take your time to choose wisely, and remember, the best friendships aren't just about being there for the good times; they're about thriving together, learning from each other, and building connections that last a lifetime. Now, armed with the know-how on what makes a great friend and how to spot the not-so-great ones, you're set to build your own epic squad. Let the adventures begin!

Quiz Choosing Friends - Qualities of Good Friendships

1. What's one of the first steps in choosing good friends?

   a) Picking the person with the coolest collection of rubber ducks
   b) Identifying your core values, like a knight with a code of honor
   c) Seeing who can burp the alphabet the fastest

2. Which trait is essential in a good friend?

   a) Reliability, like a trusty old bike that never gets a flat tire
   b) Inconsistency, like a magician's disappearing rabbit
   c) Disrespect, like a cat knocking things off the table for fun

3. What's a red flag to watch out for in a potential friend?

   a) Consistency in baking delicious cookies
   b) Disrespecting your boundaries, like a nosy alien
   c) Supporting your individuality, like a cheerleading unicorn

4. Why is diversity in friendships important?

   a) It makes your group photo look like a rainbow exploded
   b) It enriches your life with new ideas and experiences, like adding spices to a friendship stew
   c) It ensures everyone agrees that pineapple belongs on pizza

5. How can you tell if someone is a supportive friend?

   a) They only talk about their pet hamster's adventures
   b) They celebrate your achievements with confetti and pom-poms
   c) They ignore your feelings like a robot programmed for world domination

Answer Key:

1. b) Identifying your core values, like a knight with a code of honor
2. a) Reliability, like a trusty old bike that never gets a flat tire
3. b) Disrespecting your boundaries, like a nosy alien
4. b) It enriches your life with new ideas and experiences, like adding spices to a friendship stew
5. b) They celebrate your achievements with confetti and pom-poms

~

DAY 22: BEING A GOOD FRIEND: RESPONSIBILITIES AND REWARDS

Friendships aren't just about having someone to share your fries with or binge-watch the latest series; they're about giving and taking, being there during the rough patches, and celebrating the wins like they're your own. Understanding the dynamics of friendship can sometimes feel like creating a piece of art, where every brushstroke influences the final masterpiece. Let's explore some of the crucial elements that make friendships not just survive but thrive.

Think of friendship as a two-way street where both sides contribute and receive—sort of like a game of catch. You throw the ball, and they catch and throw it back. If you're constantly throwing the ball and it never comes back, that's going to be one boring game, right? That's why giving and taking in friendships is vital. It's about balancing what you offer and what you get. Maybe you're great at listening, and your friend is hilarious and always lifts your spirits. What matters here isn't to keep a ledger but to feel that there's a balance over time, that your efforts and theirs harmonize to create a friendship that's rewarding for both of you. It's about contributing to the friendship willingly without tallying up who did what last. This spontaneous, generous sharing of time, energy, and pizza slices is what solidifies your bond.

Now, let's talk about being there during the tough times. Supporting a friend in need doesn't mean you have to have all the answers or fix their problems. Sometimes, it's about being present, offering a listening ear, or just sitting with them in silence. Listening is a superpower in friendships. It involves really hearing what they're saying without planning your subsequent response or comparing their problems to yours. It's about acknowledging their feelings without rushing to judge or offer unsolicited advice. If they need more than a listening ear, ask how you can help. Maybe they need help studying, a companion for a problematic errand, or just someone to binge-watch their comfort show with. Remember, the aim is not to be their hero but their friend— one who's present but not overbearing.

Celebrating your friends' successes is like cheering for your favorite team—not because you expect something in return, but because their happiness genuinely makes you happy. It could be as big as them winning a national championship or as simple as nailing a tough math test. The act of celebrating each other's achievements creates shared moments of joy, strengthening your connection and deepening your bond. It tells your friend, "I'm with you, and I'm for you," and let's face it, who doesn't want a cheerleader in their corner? These celebrations can be small gestures, like a congratulatory note, a special treat, or just a heartfelt "I'm so proud of you!" It's about recognizing their efforts and showing that what matters to them matters to you, too.

Lastly, a word on boundaries—they're the invisible lines that help each person in a friendship feel safe and respected. Boundaries can range from how often you hang out to the kind of jokes you're okay with to how much you're willing to share about personal topics. Setting and respecting these boundaries are crucial for any healthy relationship. It involves communicating your needs clearly—like saying, "I need some time alone this weekend," or "I'm not comfortable discussing that topic." It's non-negotiable that this communication is a two-way street; you should respect their boundaries just as much as you want yours to be respected. Healthy boundaries help prevent feeling overwhelmed or taken advantage of, ensuring that the friendship remains a space where both of you feel valued and respected.

Journal Prompt: Being a Good Friend: Responsibilities and Rewards

Reflect on a friendship in which you feel a good balance of give and take. Describe a recent situation in which you supported your friend, or they supported you. How did this experience strengthen your bond?

Next, think about a time when you celebrated a friend's success. How did you celebrate, and how did it make both of you feel? What are some ways you can continue to show support and celebrate your friends' achievements?

Lastly, consider the boundaries in your friendships. Are there areas where you feel comfortable setting more clear boundaries? How can you communicate these boundaries to ensure mutual respect and understanding?

Write about the responsibilities and rewards of being a good friend and how these elements contribute to thriving, fulfilling friendships.

_____

_____

_____

_____

_____

_____

_____

~⚬~

DAY 23: GROUP DYNAMICS: FINDING YOUR PLACE

Are you the one who is always planning the hangouts (hello, leader!), or perhaps you're the peacemaker when drama strikes (yep, you're the mediator)? Understanding group dynamics is like figuring out where you fit on a sports team or in a band. Everyone has a role that helps the group vibe well and achieve its goals, whether that's having a blast at prom or acing a group project.

First up, let's break down some typical roles you might find in any group. There's the leader, often the one who sets directions and gets everyone pumped. Think of them as the quarterback in football, always keeping an eye on the end zone. Then there's the mediator, the one who smooths over conflicts and keeps the peace. They're like the calm yoga instructor who keeps everyone zen. The motivator is up next, always cheering the group on and making sure everyone feels included and valued, kind of like the hype person in a rap battle. And don't forget the innovator, who's always got a million ideas and sees solutions where others see problems. Identifying your natural role in a group setting isn't just about sticking to one lane; it's about knowing how you can best contribute to the group's success and harmony.

But what if you're not sure about your role? No big deal. Try observing how you behave in different group settings. What actions feel most natural to you? Do you find yourself offering solutions, keeping spirits high, or maybe ensuring everyone sticks to the plan? These clues can hint at your natural role within the group. And remember, roles can evolve. You may start out as a follower, learning the ropes. Still, as you get more comfortable, you may become a leader or an idea generator.

Now, onto a trickier part of group dynamics—peer pressure. It's like that sneaky level in a video game where everything seems fine, and then bam, you're facing a boss fight you didn't see coming. Standing firm on your values is your best defense. It helps to have a clear sense of your morals and what you're comfortable with. This way, you're ready with your shield when someone tries to sway you into skipping class or gossiping. Practice saying no in a firm yet polite way. You could say something like, "I appreciate the invite, but I'm not really into that." Remember, true friends will respect your choices, even if they're different from theirs.

Creating an inclusive group is like hosting a party where everyone feels welcome. It starts with being a good host. Introduce people to each other, highlight common interests, and create opportunities for everyone to shine. Please pay attention to who might feel left out and make an effort to bring them into the fold. For instance, ask for their opinion if you notice someone is quiet during a group discussion. Sometimes, all it takes is a simple, "Hey, Casey, you're quiet today. What do you think?" to make someone feel seen and valued.

If you spot exclusion happening, whether it's subtle or outright, it's crucial to address it. This doesn't mean calling someone out in front of everyone (which can backfire) but instead having a private conversation about how inclusivity makes for a more substantial, happier group. Share how various thoughts and backgrounds can lead to more creative and effective collaboration. After all, a group where everyone feels included is not just a nicer place to be; it's also more successful and engaged.

Balancing individual friendships within a larger group can be like juggling. You want to spend time with everyone, but you also don't want anyone to feel like they're just part of the crowd. It's vital to nurture individual relationships within the group setting. This might mean grabbing coffee with one friend or hitting the gym with another. These one-on-one hangouts can strengthen each friendship and prevent anyone from feeling like they're lost in the group shuffle.

Sometimes, private bonds can create tension in the larger group, especially if others feel excluded or if inside jokes go too far. It's vital to be mindful of how these private bonds affect group dynamics. Strive to make everyone feel included, especially during group gatherings. Share stories or jokes that everyone can enjoy, and avoid cliques that can split the group. Remember, a tight-knit group isn't about everyone being best friends with each other; it's about everyone feeling respected and included in the collective adventure.

Activity: Finding Your Place in Group Dynamics

Superhero Reflection - Think about a recent group activity or project you were part of. Reflect on your behavior. Imagine your role as a superhero persona. Write a short paragraph about your "superpowers" in the group. For example, if you're a Leader, you might be "Captain Direction," always steering the team toward success.

Peer Pressure Comic - Draw a simple comic strip showing a scenario where you face peer pressure (e.g., being pushed to skip class). Include your superhero persona standing firm against the pressure. Use speech bubbles to write your response.

Inclusivity Challenge - Plan an "Inclusivity Scavenger Hunt" for your next group activity. Create a list of actions to include everyone, such as:

- Ask a quiet member their opinion.
- Invite everyone to join a group game.
- Compliment someone on their contribution.
- Check off each action during your group activity and see how many you can complete.

Friendship Mix-and-Match - Identify one
friend in your group you haven't spent
much one-on-one time with recently. Plan a
fun, creative activity with them, like baking
cookies, going on a mini adventure, or
creating a playlist together. Give your plan a
catchy title, like "Operation Bestie Bonding."

≈

PARTIES AND SOCIAL GATHERINGS: MINGLING LIKE A PRO

Stepping into a party can be overwhelming, but you can navigate these social scenes like a pro with a few tricks.

To join a conversation, wait for a natural break, such as after a laugh or a story, and then chime in with a light comment or question. For example, "That sounds hilarious, what happened next?" introduces you without intrusion. Exiting a chat is just as necessary; do so by expressing your move positively, "I'm off to grab some refreshments, enjoyed our chat!"

Parties require mobility. Move around to increase your visibility and accessibility, making it easier for others to approach you. Introducing yourself is critical. A simple "Hi, I'm [Your Name]," accompanied by a smile, opens the door for interaction. Engage further by asking open-ended questions or offering compliments to find common ground quickly.

Combat social anxiety by preparing mentally. Use breathing exercises to calm your nerves before social encounters and set small, achievable goals for yourself, like talking to three new people. This approach helps focus your energy away from anxiety and towards positive interactions.

Understanding both others' and your own body language enhances communication. If someone seems disengaged, give them space. Conversely, open body language from you or others usually indicates interest and receptiveness to the conversation. By mastering the art of conversation, moving with purpose, managing anxiety, and reading social cues, you'll find yourself enjoying social gatherings more, making new friends, and creating lasting memories.

$\sim$

DAY 24: COMMUNICATING IN CONFLICTS: KEEPING FRIENDSHIPS STRONG

Have you ever found yourself in the middle of a heated game where suddenly, what was a friendly match turns into a virtual battlefield? It's incredible how quickly things can spiral out of control, right? Well, conflicts in friendships can feel pretty similar. One minute, you're joking around, and the next, you're both hurling words like digital missiles. But here's the kicker: resolving conflicts doesn't have to be about winning or losing. It's about understanding, adjusting, and moving forward stronger. Let's gear up and dive into some strategies to help you keep your friendships as strong as a fortified castle, even when disagreements try to breach the walls.

First up: healthy conflict resolution. Picture this: you and your friend are at odds over which movie to watch. You're dying to watch the latest superhero flick while they're in the mood for a horror marathon. Instead of the classic "But I picked last time!" or the silent treatment, try using "I" statements. It's a game-changer. Start with, "I feel like we always end up watching what you want, and I'd really appreciate it if we could find a compromise." This way, you're expressing your feelings without blaming them and opening up the floor for a healthy discussion. It's like sending a peace envoy to negotiate terms – it keeps the doors of communication open. It reduces the chance of things getting messy.

Active listening is another vital player in this scenario. This means really listening to what they're saying, not just planning your next argument while they speak. Maybe they had a terrible day and are looking for some predictable scares to unwind. Finding a middle ground becomes easier when you understand where they're coming from. Maybe agree to watch a bit of both genres? By actively listening and responding with kindness, you turn a potential confrontation into a win-win situation, keeping the friendship on solid ground.

Now, let's tackle de-escalating arguments before they turn into full-blown wars. It's all about catching the tension early and hitting the brakes. Imagine you're in a heated discussion that's rapidly going south. Suggest taking a timeout instead of throwing fuel on the fire with sarcastic remarks or hurtful comments. Literally say, "Let's take a few minutes to cool down." It's like hitting the pause button on a tense gameplay, giving both of you time to breathe and collect your thoughts. When emotions are running high, stepping back can prevent saying things you might regret and helps maintain the respect that's so crucial in any relationship.

After cooling down, approaching the discussion with a clear, calm mind can make a huge difference. Think of it as re-entering the game with a new strategy after realizing the old one wasn't working. Discuss calmly and clearly what bothered you, listen to the other person's side, and try to find a solution that respects both perspectives. Sometimes, just the act of calmly discussing an issue can make all the difference, turning a potential friendship-ending argument into a moment of mutual understanding and respect.

Moving on is part of any strong friendship: the ability to apologize and forgive. Let's say you dropped the ball — maybe you forgot their birthday or accidentally spilled a secret. Owning up to your mistakes and offering a sincere apology can go a long way. A simple, heartfelt "I'm really sorry I hurt you; that wasn't my intention" shows maturity and respect for the friendship. It's about acknowledging your blunder and showing that you care enough to make amends.

On the flip side, forgiving a friend who genuinely apologizes is equally important. Holding onto grudges is like lugging a heavy backpack during a hike; it just makes the journey more challenging. Forgiving doesn't mean forgetting; it means choosing to move forward. It helps rebuild trust and respect, which are the foundation of any strong relationship. Remember, everyone makes mistakes, and forgiveness is a gift that heals both the giver and the receiver.

Finally, let's talk about turning lemons into lemonade. Conflicts, when handled properly, can actually strengthen friendships. They're like the challenging moments in a group project that push you to work together and improve. Each disagreement gives you insights into each other's boundaries, expectations, and communication styles. For instance, you might learn that your friend hates being teased in public or that they need some time to think before discussing an issue. These insights are valuable; they help you understand each other better, paving the way for a more considerate and connected relationship.

So, next time you find yourself in a disagreement, look at it as an opportunity to improve your friendship. Discuss openly what you both can learn from the experience and how you can prevent similar conflicts in the future. Maybe you establish a code word that means, "This is important to me; let's discuss this calmly," or you always agree to take a break and revisit the conversation with a clear mind. These strategies not only solve the immediate problem but also bolster your friendship against future storms, making sure that your ship sails smoothly even when the waters get rough.

Quiz: Communicating in Conflicts - Keeping Friendships Strong

1. What's a healthy way to start a discussion when you and a friend disagree on what movie to watch?

    a) "Rock, paper, scissors for the win!"
    b) "I feel like we always end up watching what you want. Can we compromise?"
    c) "I'm building a fort, and it's superhero-themed. Join or be banished!"

2. What's the best approach when your friend is talking about their bad day and you're in a disagreement?

    a) Interrupt with, "Hey, let's talk about me now!"
    b) Actively listen and respond with kindness.
    c) Pretend you're a detective solving a mystery: "Interesting, tell me more about this 'terrible day.'"

3. How can you de-escalate a heated argument with a friend?

    a) Suggest a timeout and take a few minutes to cool down.
    b) Challenge them to a thumb war to settle it.

c) Start a dance-off to release the tension.

4. What's an important step when you realize you've made a mistake and hurt your friend?

   a) Apologize sincerely: "I'm really sorry I hurt you.
   That wasn't my intention."
   b) Blame your imaginary twin for the mistake.
   c) Distract them with a magic trick: "Look over here,
   nothing up my sleeve!"

5. Why is forgiving a friend who apologizes important?

   a) It restores trust and helps move forward.
   b) It gives you a free pass to tease them about it
   forever.
   c) It's a perfect opportunity to invent a new secret
   handshake.

Answer Key:

1. b) "I feel like we always end up watching what you
   want. Can we compromise?"
2. b) Actively listen and respond with kindness.
3. a) Suggest a timeout and take a few minutes to cool
   down.
4. a) Apologize sincerely: "I'm really sorry I hurt you.
   That wasn't my intention."
5. a) It restores trust and helps move forward.

∽

DAY 25: WHEN TO WALK AWAY: RECOGNIZING TOXIC RELATIONSHIPS

Let's face it: Not all friendships are meant to last forever, but that's okay. It's like clearing out your playlist; sometimes, you have to remove a few tracks that no longer make you feel good. Recognizing when a friendship turns toxic—meaning it consistently drains your happiness or undermines your well-being—is crucial for maintaining your mental health. A toxic relationship can be laced with manipulation, constant negativity, or disrespect. These aren't just bad days that everyone has; these are patterns that make you feel worse after every interaction. A friend who manipulates you might twist your words, make you feel guilty for things that aren't your fault, or even try to control your decisions. Persistent negativity from a friend can look like constant criticism, cynicism about your dreams, or pitting you against your own values. Disrespect might come through in dismissive behaviors, ignoring your boundaries, or ridiculing your interests. Recognizing these traits is the first step in protecting your well-being.

Now, how do you know when it's time to walk away? Imagine your energy as a battery—some interactions might recharge you, while others could drain you dry. If you consistently feel depleted after hanging out with someone or if you notice your self-esteem dropping faster than your phone's battery life, those are big red flags. Another sign is if you find your boundaries being repeatedly trampled. For instance, if you've expressed discomfort about certain jokes and they keep making them anyway, that's a clear sign of disrespect. Trust your gut here. If something feels off, it probably is. Lack of trust is another deal-breaker. If you're second-guessing their intentions more often than not, or if you think you can't rely on them in the moments it matters, the foundation of your friendship might be shaky.

Ending a friendship, especially a long-standing one, can feel as daunting as quitting a long-term job. You might worry about the aftermath or whether you're making the right decision. However, just like in any breakup, clarity and respect are a must-have. Plan what you want to say beforehand. You might start with something like, "I've been feeling [insert feelings] about our friendship for a while, and I think it's best for me to step back." Be honest, but also be compassionate. You're not trying to win an argument but to close a section peacefully. Stick to "I" statements to express your feelings without unnecessarily blaming the other person. This isn't about their character flaws; it's about how the relationship isn't working for you.

After you've parted ways, it's necessary to dive into some serious self-care. Think of it as emotional first aid. This could be anything from spending time with people who recharge your batteries to picking up hobbies that you might have put aside. Allow yourself to grieve the loss of the friendship. It's okay to feel sad, confused, or even relieved. Processing these emotions is part of healing. Don't rush into new friendships right away. Give yourself the space to understand what went wrong and what you truly value in friendships. This reflection will help you build healthier friendships in the future, ones that uplift and support you just as much as you do them.

Navigating friendships isn't always straightforward. It involves a lot of trial and error, adjustments, and sometimes, tough decisions like ending a friendship. However, each interaction, each connection, and each conclusion teaches you more about who you are and what you value in relationships. As you move forward, you'll find that the friendships that do stick around are those that bring out the best in you and you in them.

Journal Prompt: When to Walk Away: Recognizing Toxic Relationships

Reflect on a friendship that has made you feel consistently unhappy or drained. Write about specific behaviors or patterns that have made you feel this way. How have these interactions impacted your well-being and self-esteem?

Next, consider the signs that suggest it might be time to walk away from this friendship. Do you feel your boundaries are being ignored or your trust is consistently broken?

Finally, think about how you would approach ending this friendship. What would you say to express your feelings honestly and respectfully?

Write down some self-care strategies you can use to help you heal and process the end of this friendship. How will you ensure your future friendships are healthy and supportive?

_____

_____

_____

_____

_____

MANAGING CONFLICT: REAL-LIFE STRATEGIES FOR TOUGH SITUATIONS

Conflict is an inevitable part of life, much like an uninvited party guest. It can arise from minor disagreements to major arguments, but you can navigate these challenges effectively with the right strategies.

Assertive communication is needed in resolving conflicts. It involves expressing your thoughts, feelings and needs transparently, openly, and respectfully. Instead of accusing others with "You" statements, use "I" statements to focus on how you feel and what you need. For example, swap "You never listen to me" with "I feel unheard when I'm interrupted." This approach fosters understanding and empathy, paving the way for real solutions.

Aim for win-win solutions where all parties feel they've gained something. Understand the other person's perspective to identify mutual needs and concerns. Be creative in brainstorming solutions that accommodate everyone involved. Whether it's negotiating car usage with a sibling or dividing tasks in a group project, finding common ground is imperative.

Staying calm under pressure is essential. If emotions run high, take a timeout. A brief pause can help you cool down, think clearly, and return to the discussion with a more focused perspective. Managing your emotions prevents minor disagreements from escalating.

After resolving a conflict, reflect on the experience. Consider what triggered the disagreement, how you managed it, and what you learned. This reflection isn't about dwelling on mistakes but about preparing for future conflicts. Every situation offers insights to improve your conflict-resolution skills. In learning to handle conflicts constructively, you not only maintain but also strengthen relationships. Communicating assertively, seeking mutually beneficial solutions, managing emotions, and reflecting on your experiences are all significant steps. Embrace these opportunities for growth and understanding, and approach each conflict as a chance to develop your skills.

Up next, we'll explore how to develop romantic relationships, another complex but rewarding part of your social journey.

As branches intertwine, they symbolize the bonds of friendship —strong, supportive, and ever-growing. The tree shows how these connections, rooted in trust and shared experiences, help it weather any storm.

SECTION 7 DEVELOPING ROMANTIC RELATIONSHIPS

"We accept the love we think we deserve."

STEPHEN CHBOSKY, THE PERKS OF
BEING A WALLFLOWER

I magine you're standing in front of a giant, colorful vending machine, but it's filled with feelings instead of snacks. You put in a coin, press a button, and out pops an emotion. Surprise! You've just selected "Attraction." But wait, what exactly did you get? Is it the fizzy, exciting kind that makes your stomach do somersaults, or is it the deep, soulful variety that feels like a warm blanket on a cold day? Understanding attraction, especially as a teen, can feel a bit like trying to understand a new app—there's a lot going on, and not all of it makes sense at first glance. So let's decode this app of attraction together, shall we?

～

UNDERSTANDING ATTRACTION: MORE THAN JUST FEELINGS

Diving into the science behind attraction, it's fascinating to learn that our brains release a mix of chemicals like dopamine, oxytocin, and adrenaline when we're drawn to someone. These not only make us feel euphoric and attached but also cause physical reactions such as a racing heart. Beyond biology, emotional attraction plays a significant role, influenced by our experiences, personality, and even our mood during the initial meeting. This explains why we might feel a strong pull towards someone who doesn't fit our typical "type."

Attraction has different layers, including the physical, emotional, and intellectual. While physical attraction focuses on appearance, emotional attraction is about being drawn to someone's personality, and intellectual attraction sparks from shared interests or exciting conversations. These attractions can grow and change, transforming initial physical interest into deeper emotional connections as we get to know someone better.

Distinguishing between attraction and love is paramount; attraction is the initial interest that draws us to someone, while love is a deeper, more committed connection that values the person's well-being and accepts their flaws. Recognizing this difference can guide our decisions in pursuing relationships or appreciating a crush for the excitement it brings.

To manage attraction effectively, it's important to keep perspective and not let it consume your life. Slow down to truly understand your feelings and the nature of your attraction, communicate openly, and reflect on what you appreciate about the person beyond just their appearance.

Managing attraction thoughtfully is fundamental in developing healthy, fulfilling relationships and understanding ourselves and our partnership values.

"Love is not about how much you say 'I love you,' but how much you can prove that it's true."

UNKNOWN

DAY 26: HEALTHY DATING PRACTICES: RESPECT AND CONSENT

So, you're considering stepping into the dating scene, or maybe you're already knee-deep in it. Either way, navigating the waters of romantic relationships is a bit like learning to drive. There are rules to follow, signals to understand, and it's necessary to respect the other 'drivers' on the road. Let's break down the essentials of healthy dating practices, which are all about respect, honesty, and, of course, a good dose of mutual understanding.

Diving headfirst into dating without understanding the basics of respectful relationships is like trying to run before you can walk—it's likely to lead to some trips and falls. The cornerstone of any healthy relationship is respect. This means valuing each other's opinions, feelings, and boundaries. It's about listening to your partner and treating their views with the same level of importance as your own. Honesty plays a huge role, too. Being upfront about your feelings and intentions sets the stage for a clear and trusting relationship. This isn't just about avoiding lies; it's about being open about what you're looking for in a relationship, whether it's something casual or more serious.

Consideration is another big one. Understanding and caring for each other's emotional and physical well-being can make all the difference. This means being mindful of what makes your partner comfortable and what doesn't and never intentionally pushing those boundaries. It's about making sure that the relationship is a space where both of you feel safe, valued, and heard. Think of it as a two-player game where both players need to be enjoying themselves for the game to continue successfully.

Now, let's talk about the most indispensable must-have in any relationship: consent. Consent in dating, just like in any other situation, is all about agreement and voluntary participation. It's crucial in all aspects of dating, from holding hands to kissing to everything else that couples do. Consent should always be explicit, enthusiastic, and ongoing. This means you need to check in with your partner before moving to a new level in your relationship. A simple "Is this okay?" can go a long way. And remember, consent, once given, can be withdrawn at any time; it's not a one-time checkbox.

Teaching teens like yourself how to give, recognize, and respect consent is vital. It helps build relationships on foundations of mutual respect and care. Plus, understanding consent fully prepares you for interactions not just with romantic partners but in all areas of life. It's about confirming that all parties are always comfortable with what's happening and that no one feels pressured or forced.

Clear communication is the backbone of any strong relationship, and part of that communication involves setting expectations. This isn't about laying down rules for each other but rather about sharing what you both hope to get out of the relationship. It's like setting the terms before starting a group project—you want to make sure everyone's on the same page and agrees with the plan. Talk about how often you expect to see each other, what your ideas of a perfect date might be, and how you view your relationship growing. These conversations can help prevent misunderstandings and ensure that both partners feel comfortable and respected.

Lastly, peer pressure. It's like the annoying pop-up ads of your social life; it's there, and you have to deal with it, but you don't have to click on it. As a teen, you might feel pressure to start dating, engage in physical intimacy, or stay in a relationship that feels wrong just because it seems like everyone else is doing it. The key here is to stick to your personal values and comfort levels. Remember, dating is personal and subjective. What works for someone else might not work for you, and that's perfectly okay. If you feel pressured, talk about it with someone you trust—a friend, a family member, or a counselor. They can offer you perspective and support, helping you to stand firm in your decisions.

Navigating dating as a teen is no small feat—it's filled with excitement, new experiences, and, of course, its fair share of challenges. By building your relationships on the foundations of respect, honesty, and consent, setting clear expectations, and managing peer pressure, you're setting yourself up for healthier and happier romantic experiences. Remember, every relationship, just like every person, is unique. Take things at your own pace, respect yourself and your partner, and don't be afraid to speak up for what you believe in or need.

Quiz: Understanding Consent in Romantic Relationships

1. What does consent mean in a romantic relationship?

a) Guessing your partner's feelings
b) Clearly and willingly agreeing to a specific activity
c) Doing whatever you think they want

2. When should you ask for consent?

a) Only the first time you do something new
b) Every time, before engaging in any activity
c) Once you've been dating for a month

3. What should you do if your partner says "no" to an activity?

a) Respect their decision and stop immediately
b) Try to persuade them to change their mind
c) Ignore it and proceed anyway

4. Can consent be withdrawn after it has been given?

a) Yes, at any time
b) No, once given, it can't be taken back
c) Only in certain situations

5. Which of these is an example of explicit consent?

a) Silence
b) A hesitant "maybe"
c) An enthusiastic "yes"

6. What is not a valid reason to assume consent?

a) They agreed to something similar before
b) They haven't said "no"
c) They are smiling and seem comfortable

7. What should you do if your partner looks uncomfortable but hasn't said anything?

    a) Continue and hope they're okay with it

    b) Stop and ask if they're comfortable

    c) Assume they're fine since they haven't objected

8. Why is it important to talk about boundaries and consent in a relationship?

    a) To ensure both partners feel safe and respected

    b) To avoid misunderstandings

    c) Both a and b

9. Can someone give consent if they are under the influence of alcohol or drugs?

    a) Yes, as long as they say "yes"

    b) No, being under the influence affects their ability to consent

    c) Only if they're not too drunk

10. What's the best way to ensure ongoing consent in a relationship?

    a) Check in regularly with your partner and communicate openly

    b) Assume it's always there once established

    c) Only ask when you're unsure

Answer Key:

  1. b) Clearly and willingly agreeing to a specific activity

  2. b) Every time, before engaging in any activity

3. a) Respect their decision and stop immediately
4. a) Yes, at any time
5. c) An enthusiastic "yes"
6. b) They haven't said "no"
7. b) Stop and ask if they're comfortable
8. c) Both a and b
9. b) No, being under the influence affects their ability to consent
10. a) Check in regularly with your partner and communicate openly

∾

DAY 27: SELF-RESPECT IN RELATIONSHIPS: SETTING BOUNDARIES

So, you're in a relationship, or maybe eyeing one, and you're buzzing with all those feel-good vibes. But let's hit pause for a sec and talk about something super crucial—boundaries. Think of boundaries like your personal rule book; these are your dos and don'ts that help you navigate through relationship waters without losing yourself. It's not about building walls but rather drawing your lines clearly in the sand. Whether it's how much time you spend together, how you handle personal space, or what's cool to share online, setting these personal guidelines is a top priority to keeping any relationship healthy and happy.

Okay, first things first: figuring out your own boundaries. This is about knowing what you're comfortable with physically, emotionally, and digitally. Physically, it might be about how affectionate you are or your comfort level with PDA (public displays of affection). Emotionally, it's about knowing how much of your own feelings and thoughts you're ready to share. And digitally? Well, it's the 21st century, so think about things like whether you're okay with being Instagram official or how much you want to text. Everyone's comfort levels are different, so take some time to think about what feels right for you. Maybe jot down a list or chat about it with a friend to get your thoughts organized.

Now, having boundaries is great, but if they're just rolling around in your head, they're not doing much good. You've got to communicate them to your partner. And nope, this isn't a one-and-done kind of deal; it's an ongoing conversation because relationships evolve, and so might your boundaries. Start the chat with something like, "Hey, can we talk about what we're cool within our relationship?" Keep the tone positive and constructive. It's not about listing demands but rather sharing what makes you feel comfortable and respected. Remember, it's a dialogue, not a monologue, so be ready to listen to their boundaries too.

Once the boundaries are out in the open, respecting them is necessary. It's like each of you has given the other a roadmap to your comfort zones, and it's imperative to stick to the path. If your partner respects your boundaries, awesome! It shows they care about your feelings and comfort. But hey, we're all human, and sometimes people might slip up. If something feels off, gently reminding them about your boundaries is okay. Say something like, "I mentioned before that I'm not cool with that. Can we try another way?" It's all about maintaining respect and understanding that helps both of you feel secure and valued.

But what if the boundary crossings aren't just slip-ups but more of a regular thing? That's where things get a bit more serious. It's essential to assert yourself and remind your partner that your boundaries are non-negotiable. Be clear and firm but also calm. If the boundary-pushing continues, it might be time to seek advice from someone you trust, like a friend, family member, or counselor. They can offer you a fresh perspective and support. Sometimes, if boundaries keep getting ignored, it might even mean reviewing the relationship. Remember, a relationship should bring joy and support into your life, not stress and discomfort.

Navigating boundaries isn't always straightforward, and it can feel a bit awkward at first. But think of it as a central part of any healthy relationship. It's about giving yourself and your partner the space to be yourselves while also growing together. So, take the time to define, communicate, and respect each other's boundaries. By doing so, you're not just building a relationship but also mutual respect and understanding that will help your partnership thrive in the long run. And remember, in any relationship, your feelings and comfort matter just as much as the other person's. So, don't be afraid to speak up. Your boundaries deserve to be respected.

Journal Prompt: Self-Respect in Relationships: Setting Boundaries

Reflect on your personal boundaries in relationships. What physical, emotional, and digital boundaries are essential to you?

Write about a time when you successfully communicated your boundaries. How did you approach the conversation, and what was the outcome?

Consider a situation where your boundaries were not respected. How did you handle it, and what did you learn from the experience?

Finally, list ways you can respect your partner's boundaries. How can you ensure mutual respect and understanding in your relationship?

_____

_____

_____

_____

_____

_____

DAY 28: BALANCING ROMANCE AND FRIENDSHIPS: KEEPING LIFE IN HARMONY

When you start dating someone, it can feel like you've just got your hands on the latest, most exciting video game. Suddenly, every free moment is spent trying to level up in this new relationship. But hold up! What about your squad, the friends who've been with you through thick and thin? It's easy to get so caught up in the whirlwind of a new romance that you might unintentionally sideline your pals. Remember, maintaining a balance between your romantic relationships and friendships isn't just nice; it's necessary. It contributes massively to your overall happiness and stability. Think about it: when your romantic world gets a bit too intense or challenging, who's there to offer a different viewpoint or just a fun distraction? Yep, your friends.

Navigating the delicate art of time management between your partner and your buddies is crucial. It's about giving both your romantic relationships and friendships the time and energy they deserve. Start by looking at your weekly routine—how much time are you dedicating to your significant other versus your friends? Is there a balance, or is one side tipping the scales too much? Consider setting specific days or evenings for friend hangouts and date nights. This way, everyone knows they have their special time with you, and you avoid the pitfalls of last-minute cancellations that can leave someone feeling like a backup plan. Also, communicate openly with both your partner and your friends about your scheduling. Honesty here can prevent misunderstandings and assure all parties that they're valued in your life.

Now, let's chat about the green-eyed monster—jealousy. It can sneak into either type of relationship, stirring up drama. Maybe your friends miss the old days when you were more available, or perhaps your partner feels threatened by your close friendships. Here's where your communication skills need to shine. Address jealousy by bringing it out into the open. If a friend expresses jealousy about the time you're spending with your partner, acknowledge their feelings and reassure them of their importance in your life.

On the other hand, if your partner is feeling uneasy about your friendships, reassure them but also assert your right to have these relationships. It's about validating feelings without compromising your boundaries. Strategies like inviting your partner to join in with your friends sometimes help bridge the gap between your romantic and social lives.

Speaking of which, integrating your significant other into your wider social circles can feel like mixing two different friend groups and hoping they hit it off. Start by choosing neutral, low-pressure settings—think group outings like a beach day or a casual dinner. This allows your partner and your friends to meet on common ground without the pressure to bond instantly. Share with both parties what you value about each of them beforehand; this can pave the way for mutual respect and shared interests to appear naturally. Remember, not everyone has to be best buddies, but mutual respect and friendliness can go a long way in maintaining harmony in your interconnected relationships.

Balancing the scales between your romantic and friend relationships isn't about dividing your time evenly—it's about making sure that the time spent with each is meaningful and satisfying. It's ensuring that you nourish all aspects of your social life without letting one overshadow the other. By fostering this balance, you're not just maintaining relationships; you're enriching them, allowing each to blossom and bring out the best in you. So, as you navigate these dynamics, keep the lines of communication open, prioritize fairness in how you allocate your time, and remember, a well-rounded life includes both great friends and great loves.

Quiz: How to Balance Romance and Friendships

1. What's the first step in managing your time between a romantic partner and friends?

    a) Spend all your free time with your partner
    b) Look at your weekly routine and allocate time
    for both
    c) Ignore your friends until they complain

2. How can you ensure your friends don't feel sidelined when you start dating someone new?

   a) Set specific days or evenings for friend hangouts
   b) Only hang out with friends when your partner is busy
   c) Cancel plans with friends if your partner calls

3. What's a good way to handle jealousy from friends or your partner?

   a) Ignore their feelings and hope it goes away
   b) Address it openly and reassure them of their importance
   c) Avoid the topic and spend more time alone

4. How can you integrate your significant other into your social circles?

   a) Force them to become best friends with your friends
   b) Choose neutral, low-pressure group outings
   c) Keep your partner and friends completely separate

5. Why is balancing your romantic and friend relationships important?

   a) To ensure that your partner and friends feel equally valued
   b) To prevent feeling overwhelmed by any one relationship
   c) Both a and b

Answer Key:

1. b) Look at your weekly routine and allocate time for both
2. a) Set specific days or evenings for friend hangouts
3. b) Address it openly and reassure them of their importance
4. b) Choose neutral, low-pressure group outings
5. c) Both a and b

DEALING WITH BREAKUPS: HEALTHY WAYS TO MOVE ON

Breakups feel like stepping on a LEGO—unexpected and painful. Yet, like challenging levels in a video game, they test our skills and contribute to our growth. Here's how to navigate them with resilience and even gain some insights.

Feeling a whirlwind of emotions is normal post-breakup. It's imperative to express these feelings—through journaling, talking with friends, or even screaming into a pillow. Acknowledge your feelings without dwelling on them too long. Recognize, understand, and gently remind yourself that moving forward is part of the process.

Self-care is a must-have. Maintain your routine, including school and hobbies, and keep a regular sleep schedule. Lean on your support system and try new activities that excite you. Remember, seeking professional help is also a form of self-care, offering additional support when needed.

Every breakup teaches us valuable lessons. Reflect on the relationship to understand your needs and areas for personal growth. This reflection isn't about blame but about learning more about yourself and your desires in a relationship.

Moving on means opening yourself to new possibilities and using the lessons learned to brighten your future. The right time to move on varies for each person. Listen to yourself and move at a pace that feels right for you, ensuring you're moving on for the right reasons. Navigating breakups is hard but also a chance for personal growth. By healthily processing emotions, practicing self-care, learning from the experience, and knowing when you're ready to move on, you're laying the foundation for stronger, healthier future relationships. Remember, each step forward is a step towards a happier, more fulfilled you. As we close this section, we're reminded that life's challenges, including breakups, are pivotal in shaping us into the individuals we're meant to become. Next, we'll delve into handling rejection and failure, continuing to build resilience and confidence.

When the tree bears fruit, it reflects the culmination of nurturing relationships. Just as fruit develops from the union of blossoms and branches, romantic relationships grow from shared care, trust, and mutual growth.

SECTION 8 HANDLING REJECTION AND FAILURE

> "I've missed more than 9,000 shots in my career. I've lost almost 300 games. Twenty-six times, I've been trusted to take the game-winning shot and missed. I've failed over and over and over again in my life. And that is why I succeed."
>
> MICHAEL JORDAN

Ever felt like you're stuck in a never-ending audition for the role of "punching Bag' in the blockbuster movie of life, where every rejection hits like an unexpected plot twist? Well, you're not alone in this script. Rejection, whether it's from a crush who ghosted you, a college that sent a rejection letter instead of an acceptance, or friends who traded you for the cool table, rejection can feel like the ultimate plot twist. But here's a little spoiler: it's not really about you. Let's peel back the curtain and see rejection for what it really is—a mismatch of circumstances, not a critique of your awesomeness.

IT'S NOT PERSONAL: UNDERSTANDING REJECTION AND FAILURE

Rejection is not a reflection of your worth; it is more like a USB plug not fitting the right port. It's about compatibility, not value. Understanding this helps diminish the sting of rejection, transforming a potentially soul-crushing moment into a simple mismatch to shrug off.

Whether it's being ignored by a crush, left out by friends, or facing academic disappointments, these experiences, although challenging, serve as redirections toward paths more aligned with your journey. They're not stop signs but detours to better-suited avenues.

To manage the emotional whirlwind that rejection can bring, it's imperative to shift your perspective. Instead of seeing it as a sign of personal inadequacy, try to view it as a situational mismatch. Mindfulness exercises can also help by teaching you to acknowledge and observe your feelings without letting them overwhelm you.

Your value isn't defined by external validations like making a team or getting into a specific college. Grounding your self-esteem in your strengths, talents, and meaningful relationships helps you stay resilient. Remember, you are much more than your rejections or failures.

View failure as 'Growth Fuel' rather than a setback. Every failure offers insights, offering you a chance to learn, tweak, and improve. Analyze your failures constructively, focusing on what you can learn rather than dwelling on the negative.

Use your failures as lessons to guide your future actions. If public speaking makes you nervous, join a debate club. If procrastination is your downfall, set gradual goals. It's about applying lessons learned to do better next time.

Risk-taking and experimentation foster growth. Embracing challenges and stepping out of your comfort zone can lead to significant learning opportunities. Every attempt, regardless of its outcome, enriches your understanding and skills. Remember, failure is not the enemy but a guide towards growth and resilience. It's the setbacks that pave the way for comebacks. Keep pushing forward, learning, and daring to explore new paths. Your story is defined not by the failures you encounter but by how you respond to them.

DAY 29: SEEKING FEEDBACK: GROWTH FROM CRITICISM

Feedback is like the secret sauce that can turn your plain old burger of efforts into a gourmet masterpiece. But let's be real; it can sometimes taste a bit bitter. The trick is to start seeing feedback as your ally, not your enemy—it's the coach, not the critic. Adopting a positive attitude towards feedback can be a game-changer in your personal and professional growth. Think of it as getting the cheat codes to level up faster and smarter. It's not about someone pointing out your faults; it's about getting insights that can propel you forward. So, how do you turn feedback into your growth superpower? Let's break it down.

First up, getting good at asking for feedback is like learning to mine gold—you need to know where to dig and what tools to use. Start by identifying who to ask. Your best bet is people who regularly observe your performance and whose opinions you respect. This could be a teacher, coach, or even a friend who isn't afraid to give you the real talk. Once you've spotted your feedback providers, it's all about how you frame your request. Instead of a vague "Do you think I did okay?" try a more targeted approach, like, "What's one thing I could improve in my presentations?" Specific questions like this make it easier for people to offer helpful, precise advice rather than general 'good job' platitudes.

Now, receiving feedback can sometimes feel like swallowing a spoonful of wasabi—intense and uncomfortable. However, the real skill lies in interpreting this feedback effectively. Not all feedback will be valuable, and it's crucial to distinguish constructive criticism from less helpful comments. Constructive feedback usually focuses on specific behaviors or actions. It includes suggestions for improvement rather than just pointing out what's wrong. For example, a comment like, "You tend to speak really fast during presenta-tions, which can make it hard to follow," is actionable. It highlights a specific area of improvement rather than just saying, "Your presentation wasn't good."

Once you've sifted through the feedback and picked out the golden nuggets of constructive criticism, the next step is to create an action plan. This is where you turn insight into action. Say you've been told you need to boost your engage-ment in team projects. Set yourself a goal like, "In the next group project, I will contribute at least three new ideas and ask for feedback from my peers at least twice." Make your goals SMART—Specific, Measurable, Achievable, Relevant, and Time-bound. This approach not only structures your efforts but also makes it easier to track your progress.

Lastly, feedback should be a loop, not a one-off. After imple-menting the changes based on the initial feedback, go back and ask for more. It's like a game where each level you complete gives you the skills to tackle the next one. Keep the feedback loop going, and you'll find that each round of advice and adjustments brings you closer to mastering the skills you're working on. This ongoing process not only improves your abilities but also deepens your understanding of how you can continue to grow and adapt over time.

In the grand scheme of things, seeking and using feedback effectively are required to turn criticism into stepping stones for success. By learning how to ask the right questions, interpreting the feedback accurately, and taking actionable steps based on the advice, you set yourself up for continuous improvement and success. Remember, every piece of feedback is a perspective that can help you refine your skills and strategies, ensuring that you're not just moving forward but also upward. So next time you get a chance, reach out for that feedback and turn it into your ladder to new heights.

Journal Prompt: Seeking Feedback: Growth from Criticism

Reflect on a recent instance where you received feedback. What was the feedback about, and who provided it? How did you feel when you first received it?

Identify the constructive elements in the feedback and how you can turn them into actionable steps for improvement.

Write down a plan to seek feedback regularly. Who will you ask, and what specific questions will you pose to get valuable insights?

Consider how you can maintain a positive attitude towards feedback and use it for continuous growth. What strategies will you implement to view feedback as a tool for success?

_____

_____

_____

_____

_____

RESILIENCE BUILDING: BOUNCING BACK STRONGER

Resilience is your emotional armor, the force that propels you forward after setbacks like a bad grade, a breakup, or a rough day. It's essential for weathering life's storms, enabling you to face challenges head-on. Unlike a phone at 1% battery seeking a charger, resilience ensures you're always powered up for what life throws your way.

Cultivating resilience means embracing a growth mindset—viewing challenges as opportunities to develop rather than impossible barriers. Mistakes and failures become lessons that enhance your skills, pushing you to see beyond current obstacles.

Take inspiration from resilience icons like Malala Yousafzai and LeBron James. Malala transformed her recovery into a global advocacy for girls' education, while LeBron turned early career criticisms into a motivator for success. Their stories exemplify how resilience can convert hardships into stepping stones for advancement, not just a return to the status quo.

Building resilience is an ongoing process, with journaling as a foundational practice. It's more than airing frustrations; it's about acknowledging achievements and expressing gratitude. Regularly jotting down positive experiences shifts focus from negatives to positives, strengthening your psychological resilience. This habit acts like an emotional savings account, ready for withdrawal in tough times.

Incorporating these strategies reshapes your perspective on life's challenges, viewing them as integral to your personal growth. Whether it's finding your inner Malala or LeBron, adopting a growth mindset, or chronicling your journey through journaling, each step fortifies your resilience. Embrace every obstacle as a chance to demonstrate your strength. Keep pushing forward, grow more robust, and let resilience guide you.

~

DAY 30: MOVING FORWARD: MAINTAINING MOTIVATION AFTER A FALL

So, you've hit a bump in the road, maybe even tumbled into a metaphorical ditch along your path to greatness. It happens! The real trick isn't just getting out of the ditch; it's how you dust yourself off and keep marching toward your dreams with the same pep in your step. Keeping your eyes on the prize, or in less cliché terms, maintaining a focus on your long-term goals, can turn these temporary setbacks into mere blips on your radar. It's about seeing the bigger picture. Every stumble feels like a wall when you're fixated only on the immediate hurdles. Still, with your gaze fixed on the horizon, every fall is just one step in a much grander journey.

Think of your long-term goals as your personal North Star, guiding you through dark skies and stormy weather. Whether it's acing your exams, becoming captain of the debate team, or simply improving your social circles, these aren't just checkboxes on your to-do list; they are stepping stones to the future you are building. Keep these visions clear in your mind. Visualize achieving these goals; what does it look like? How does it feel? This isn't just daydreaming; it's a technique used by athletes, entrepreneurs, and artists alike to keep their focus laser-sharp. Visualization can be a powerful motivator, especially when the going gets tough. It's like keeping a photo of the finish line in your pocket as you run the race.

Now, let's jazz up your motivational techniques with some actionable strategies. Affirmations might sound a bit out there, but trust me, giving yourself a daily pep talk can boost your spirits and your confidence. Start your day by telling yourself something positive. It could be, "I am capable of handling whatever comes my way," or "I am continuously moving towards my goals." It's about setting a positive tone for the day and strengthening your belief in yourself. Then, break down your primary goals into smaller, bite-sized pieces. These are your short-term goals, and they should be specific and achievable. Instead of "Get better at math," try "Complete two extra math problems every day." These mini-goals are quick wins that keep your motivational fires burning. Each small victory builds your confidence and propels you further towards your larger ambitions.

But let's be honest: motivation isn't a solo journey. It's a team sport, and your support system—friends, family, mentors—

plays a role. These are the cheerleaders in your personal arena, the ones who lift you up when you're down and cheer the loudest when you succeed. Lean on them. Share your frustrations and your triumphs. Sometimes, just talking about a setback can lighten your load and open up perspectives you hadn't considered. These people believe in you; their faith can help bolster your own, especially when your spirits are flagging.

Self-compassion is another major factor in maintaining motivation. Be kind to yourself. Understand that failure is a universal experience; it doesn't single you out as unworthy or incapable. Treat yourself with the same kindness you would offer a friend in your shoes. Practice mindfulness to stay present and grounded, appreciating your efforts regardless of the outcome. Remember, being hard on yourself is like trying to grow a garden by pouring salt into the soil—it just doesn't work. Nurture your garden with patience and kindness, and watch as it returns to bloom, more vibrant than before.

So, as you move forward, remember that maintaining motivation isn't about pushing yourself relentlessly toward perfection. It's about moving confidently towards your goals, armed with a clear vision, actionable plans, and an unshakeable support network. It's about being your own biggest supporter, treating setbacks as lessons, and continuously moving forward, one step at a time.

Activity: Personal North Star Visualization

1. Sit comfortably in a quiet space where you won't be disturbed.
2. Close your eyes and take a few deep breaths to center yourself.

3. Imagine your long-term goals as clearly as possible. Picture the steps you must take to achieve them and the result.

4. Write down how achieving these goals makes you feel. Use descriptive words to capture the emotions and sensations.

5. Draw a simple image or symbol that represents your North Star (your ultimate goal). Place it somewhere you'll see daily.

As this final section closes, remember the essence of what it means to keep pushing forward. It's about more than just overcoming obstacles; it's about evolving with each experience, armed with a better understanding of yourself and a refined approach to your goals. Keep your eyes on the horizon, your support close, and your internal dialogue positive. Stay tuned, stay motivated, and, most importantly, stay true to your path. The journey continues with a bonus section, which contains three practical applications and everyday scenarios.

In autumn, the tree sheds its leaves, a natural cycle that mirrors handling rejection and failure. The shedding is not an end but a preparation for renewal, as the tree draws strength from within to emerge stronger in the next season.

definitely nothing. Your presentation with a clear main point, and end on an encouraging note like a new perspective. Don't communicate with your fidgety, smile, and nod any number of including gestures and change your content and the allotted time.

BONUS: 3 PRACTICAL APPLICATION AND EVERYDAY SCENARIOS

> "Don't let the noise of others' opinions drown out your own inner voice."

STEVE JOBS

I magine you're about to deliver a presentation in front of your class. Your palms are sweaty, and the pressure is on. It's not just any moment—it's your time to shine. Excelling in a presentation can feel as rewarding as winning a significant game. However, triumph requires skill-building first. Let's explore how to confidently communicate, engage your classmates, and manage nerves effectively.

BONUS 1: ACING SCHOOL PRESENTATIONS WITH CONFIDENCE

Think of preparing for a presentation like planning a road trip—you wouldn't start without a map, snacks, and tunes.

Similarly, outline your presentation with a clear start, middle, and end to structure your talk like a story. Practice aloud to get comfortable with your delivery, smoothing out any "umms" or awkward gestures, and ensure your content fits the allotted time.

Start with a strong hook—a surprising fact or bold statement—to capture attention. Maintain eye contact to connect with your classmates, using rhetorical questions and vivid language to keep them engaged. Avoid jargon to ensure clarity and keep your audience hooked.

Feeling nervous is natural and indicates you care. Use deep breathing to calm your mind, and visualize a successful outcome to boost confidence. Embrace the adrenaline to energize your presentation, making it more compelling.

Value feedback from teachers and peers as a tool for growth. Listen actively, seek specifics to understand your strengths and areas for improvement, and apply this insight to refine your skills. Receiving feedback is a chance to see where you shine and where to focus your efforts. Mastering school presentations goes beyond not fumbling through slides—it's about captivating your audience, managing anxiety, and leveraging feedback to enhance your communication skills. With these strategies, you're set to deliver outstanding presentations.

～

BONUS 2: NAILING YOUR FIRST JOB INTERVIEW

Stepping into your first job interview feels like the spotlight's on you, not for a performance, but for a chance to kickstart your career. Success here goes beyond luck; it's about preparation and making a memorable impression.

Start by thoroughly researching the company. Dive deep into its website to understand its projects and values. This knowledge lets you tailor your responses, showing you're not just a candidate but a potential asset who aligns with its vision. Preparation extends to anticipating interview questions. Instead of memorizing answers, craft thoughtful responses that reflect your skills and experiences, making sure they're relevant to the position. This approach turns the nerve-wracking interview questions into opportunities to showcase your strengths confidently.

First impressions begin the moment you arrive. Dress appropriately and arrive 10-15 minutes early to show your punctuality and eagerness. Greet your interviewer with a firm handshake and a friendly smile to set a positive tone from the start.

Employ the STAR technique for behavioral questions, structuring your answers to highlight your problem-solving and critical-thinking skills. STAR stands for Situation, Task, Action, and Result. Begin by describing the **Situation** you were in, then explain the **Task** you needed to accomplish. Next, outline the specific **Actions** you took to address the task, and finally, share the **Results** of those actions, emphasizing any positive outcomes. This method ensures your responses are clear, concise, and impactful.

Don't forget the follow-up. A thank-you email post-interview not only shows good manners but also reiterates your interest in the position and highlights the main points from your conversation, keeping you fresh in the interviewer's mind. Remember, acing your first job interview is about detailed preparation, making a strong initial impact, effectively structuring your answers, and thoughtful follow-up. These steps are not just about landing the job but laying the groundwork for a successful career with confidence and skill.

∾

BONUS 3: VOLUNTEERING - A PATH TO ENHANCED SOCIAL SKILLS

Volunteering is your secret level in the social skills video game. It's not just about boosting your resume; it's about making impactful contributions, enhancing teamwork, and expanding your network. Think of yourself as a matchmaker, aligning your passions with meaningful causes. Whether it's supporting animal welfare, conserving the environment, or aiding a food bank, find what ignites your passion.

Start with identifying what matters to you and then connect with organizations that share your values. Remember, the ideal match benefits both you and the cause, offering skills, friendships, and new perspectives.

Teamwork is vital in volunteering. It's about uniting diverse skills and personalities towards a common goal. Effective communication, including active listening and respectful dialogue, ensures a harmonious effort. Embrace varied roles, whether leading or following, as each offers valuable lessons. Acknowledging teammates' efforts fosters a supportive environment, motivating everyone to contribute their best.

View every volunteer opportunity as a networking event. You might meet future employers, mentors, or friends, opening doors to further opportunities. Approach each experience with professionalism and enthusiasm, making lasting impressions. Engage with a diverse group of people, learning from every interaction and potentially unlocking recommendations or introductions in your field.

Volunteering is more than accumulating service hours; it's about contributing to societal improvement. Your efforts, no matter how small, are part of a more significant movement for change. The skills and experiences gained through volunteering not only enhance your personal development but also prepare you for future challenges.

As you seek to expand your social skills, consider volunteering. It's an avenue for growth, networking, and making a real-world impact. Dive into causes you're passionate about, collaborate with teams, and connect with the community. Volunteering offers a unique platform for personal and social development.

~

REFLECTING ON GROWTH: REVIEWING YOUR 30-DAY JOURNEY

So, you've been on this wild ride for 30 days, diving deep into the social jungle, and now it's time to pull over and check your map. How far have you come? What new territories of your personality did you discover? Reflecting on your growth isn't just about giving yourself a pat on the back—it's about understanding what worked, what didn't, and how you can continue evolving. So, let's break down some nifty techniques to help you gauge your progress and plan your next moves. Think of this as your personal "level-up" checkpoint.

Self-Assessment Techniques

Self-assessment is like being your own coach. You get to ask the tough questions, cheer on the wins, and strategize over the losses. Start by revisiting the goals you set at the beginning of this guide. Did you reach them? Did they change as you progressed? This isn't just about ticking boxes; it's about understanding why some goals were met and others weren't.

For each goal, consider what skills or actions helped you succeed or what barriers stood in the way. Maybe you found that speaking up in groups became more natural with practice, or perhaps you realized that time management still trips you up. Whatever the case, each insight is a nugget of gold for your personal development stash.

To structure this reflection, you might use a simple grid method: write down each goal, what you achieved, what you learned, and what you still need to work on. This visual layout can help you see patterns in your growth and areas that need more attention. It's like a snapshot of your current skill landscape, showing you where the fertile fields lie and where the ground is still a bit rocky.

Journaling Reflections

If you've been keeping a journal these past 30 days (and if you haven't, there is no time like the present to start!), now's the time to flip back through those pages. Your journal is more than a collection of daily entries; it's a map of your mental and emotional evolution.

Look for changes in how you describe your interactions and feelings. Are you more confident in certain areas? Do you notice a shift in how you handle stress or setbacks? This isn't about judging your feelings but understanding them. It's decoding the language of your own mind and heart, which can teach you heaps about how you react and adapt to various situations.

Journaling can also highlight the moments that brought you joy, success, or pride. These are the gems that sometimes get buried in the hustle of daily challenges. Maybe you had a breakthrough in a conversation with a friend or managed a project more smoothly than ever before. Celebrate these victories! They are as much a part of your journey as the struggles.

Setting Future Goals

Now, armed with fresh insights and a clearer understanding of your strengths and weaknesses, it's time to set some new goals. But let's mix it up this time. Set some 'stretch goals' alongside your personal development goals—challenges that push you just beyond the edge of your comfort zone. If networking makes you nervous, maybe your next goal is to attend a social event or join a club. If you struggled with speaking up in class, perhaps you aim to ask or answer a question in every class for a week.

Remember, these goals should be SMART: Specific, Measurable, Achievable, Relevant, and Time-bound. This framework isn't just academic fluff; it's a proven strategy that gives your ambitions a precise shape and an actionable path. It's like programming your GPS for a new destination. You know exactly where you want to go and how you plan to get there.

Celebrating Achievements

Every step forward, no matter how small, is a step worth celebrating. Don't wait for the big wins to give yourself a high-five. Celebrated achievements fuel your journey, boosting your motivation and confidence. Maybe treat yourself to a movie night after a week of meeting your new goals, or share your progress with a friend or family member. These celebrations reinforce the positivity of your efforts and remind you that growth is not just possible; it's happening.

As you wrap up this reflection phase, remember that growth is a continuous journey, not a destination. Each day brings new challenges and opportunities to learn and improve. So, take a moment to appreciate how far you've come, and get excited about where you're headed next. The skills you've developed, the insights you've gained, and the goals you've set are all stepping stones to the next section of your personal and social development. Keep pushing forward, aiming high, and turning everyday interactions into opportunities for growth. The journey continues, and the best is yet to come!

CONCLUSION

Well, here we are at the finish line of our 30-day social skill marathon! You've sprinted through the basics of sparkling conversation, hurdled over social anxiety, and even relay-raced through the tricky tracks of digital etiquette and real-life conflicts. I hope you're feeling pumped with all the new tricks tucked into your social toolkit.

Let's do a quick victory lap around the core message of our time together: This book was all about empowering you—yes, you!—to navigate the wild world of social interactions with newfound confidence. From mastering the art of chitchat to building bridges of friendship that can withstand a bit of stormy weather, we've covered ground on improving communication, managing those stomach-churning anxious moments, and fostering a rock-solid sense of self-confidence.

Reflecting on our journey, it's clear that this wasn't just about picking up skills; it was a transformation. Each day, step by step, you've been equipped with the necessary tools not just to survive but thrive in your social universe. Whether it was handling rejection with grace or learning to listen like a pro, the growth you've experienced is designed to stick.

What are the takeaways? Remember, understanding who you are is your superpower when it comes to social interaction. Authenticity isn't just a buzzword; it's your secret weapon in making meaningful connections. Resilience, that tough cookie, will keep you going when the going gets tough. And never underestimate the power of empathy—it turns out, stepping into someone else's shoes is more than just a good stretch; it's a way to see the world in a whole new light.

On the note of individuality, let's not forget that your unique quirks and qualities aren't just extras; they're the main show. Embrace them. Rock them. Your individuality is what makes you not just part of the crowd but a standout star in it.

And hey, remember, mastering these social skills is not a 'one and done' deal. It's more like a video game; the more you play, the better you get. Keep practicing the strategies and exercises we've explored, and don't hesitate to revisit any section when you need a refresher.

Now, let's talk action! It's your turn to take these tools and start crafting your path. Improvement isn't just about knowing; it's about doing. Step out of your comfort zone, strike up a conversation, and maybe even share what you've learned with a friend who could use a boost.

And speaking of sharing, why not share your journey? Hit up your socials, chat with your peers, or even start a blog. Your challenges, successes, and insights could light the way for others on similar paths and help build a community where everyone grows together.

Thank you, truly, for joining me on this adventure. It takes guts and gusto to dive into personal growth, and by turning the pages of this book, you've shown you have plenty of both. I'm grateful for your trust and commitment.

As we close this book (literally), remember that the skills you've gained are just the beginning. The road ahead is bright with promise, and I'm excited about the incredible social journeys you're destined to have. Here's to you—confidently communicating, building meaningful connections, and expressing your most authentic self. The world is way more fun with you fully in it. Keep shining, keep sharing, and let's make every interaction count!

ACKNOWLEDGMENTS

Thank you to my editor and illustrator, Chandni Ruparel. I appreciate all of your effort and hard work making sure this book is the best that it can be.

SOURCES

American SPCC. (n.d.). *Encouraging positive online activities for kids.* Retrieved from https://americanspcc.org/encouraging-positive-online-activities-for-kids/

American University. (n.d.). *The importance of promoting digital citizenship for students.* Retrieved from https://soeonline.american.edu/blog/digital-citizenship-for-students/

Banner Health. (n.d.). *8 ways to help your teen with social anxiety face the world.* Retrieved from https://www.bannerhealth.com/healthcareblog/advise-me/ways-to-help-your-teen-with-social-anxiety-face-the-world

Better Health Channel. (n.d.). *Teenagers and communication.* Retrieved from https://www.betterhealth.vic.gov.au/health/healthyliving/teenagers-and-communication

BrainyQuote. (n.d.). *Emma Stone quotes.* Retrieved from https://www.brainyquote.com/quotes/emma_stone_817700

BrainyQuote. (n.d.). *Emma Watson quotes.* Retrieved from https://www.brainyquote.com/quotes/emma_watson_615899

Centervention. (n.d.). *Active listening exercises.* Retrieved from https://www.centervention.com/active-listening-exercises/

Child Mind Institute. (n.d.). *How to help your teen through a breakup.* Retrieved from https://childmind.org/article/how-to-help-your-teen-through-a-breakup/

Chbosky, S.** (1999). *The Perks of Being a Wallflower*. Pocket Books. "We accept the love we think we deserve."

C.S. Lewis. (1960). *The Four Loves.* HarperCollins Publishers.

Cyberbullying.org. (n.d.). *Preventing cyberbullying: Top ten tips for teens.* Retrieved from https://cyberbullying.org/preventing-cyberbullying-top-ten-tips-for-teens

ESC Region 13. (n.d.). *How to teach social skills through role-playing.* Retrieved from https://blog.esc13.net/how-to-teach-social-skills-through-role-playing/

Goodreads. (n.d.). *Taylor Swift quotes.* Retrieved from https://www.goodreads.com/quotes/374278-just-be-yourself-there-is-no-one-better

Healthline. (n.d.). *8 breathing exercises for anxiety you can try right now.* Retrieved from https://www.healthline.com/health/breathing-exercises-for-anxiety

Healthline. (n.d.). *Positive self-talk: Benefits and techniques.* Retrieved from https://www.healthline.com/health/positive-self-talk

Helpful Professor. (2024). *38 examples of SMART goals for students.* Retrieved from https://helpfulprofessor.com/smart-goals-examples-for-students/

Jobs, S. (2005, June 12). *Stanford commencement speech.* Retrieved from https://news.stanford.edu/2005/06/12/youve-got-find-love-jobs-says/

Jordan, M. (n.d.). *Quotes on success.* Widely attributed.

KidsHealth. (n.d.). *Rejection and how to handle it (for teens).* Retrieved from https://kidshealth.org/en/teens/rejection.html

Lady Wind Song. (n.d.). *The STAR method: A guide to mastering interview questions.* Retrieved from https://ladywindsong.com/5561-the-star-method-a-guide-to-mastering-interview-questions-51/

Lifehack. (n.d.). *15 highly successful people who failed before succeeding.* Retrieved from https://www.lifehack.org/articles/productivity/15-highly-successful-people-who-failed-their-way-success.html

Loveisrespect.org. (n.d.). *Self-esteem for teens: Why it matters, and how you can help.* Retrieved from https://www.loveisrespect.org/resources/self-esteem-teens-why-it-matters-how-you-can-help/

Mayo Clinic. (n.d.). *Teens and social media use: What's the impact?* Retrieved from https://www.mayoclinic.org/healthy-lifestyle/tween-and-teen-health/in-depth/teens-and-social-media-use/art-20474437

Medical News Today. (n.d.). *18 mindfulness activities for teens and students.* Retrieved from https://www.medicalnewstoday.com/articles/mindfulness-activities-for-teens

Merriam-Webster. (n.d.). *Social anxiety.* In Merriam-Webster.com dictionary. Retrieved from https://www.merriam-webster.com/dictionary/social%20anxiety

Middle Earth. (2011, January 10). *How teens can be and pick a good friend.* Retrieved from https://middleearthnj.org/2011/01/10/how-teens-can-be-and-pick-a-good-friend/

Monash University. (2023, May 1). *Building a powerful self-identity: Why it matters for adolescents.* Retrieved from https://lens.monash.edu/@education/2023/05/01/1385697/building-a-powerful-self-identity-why-it-matters-for-adolescents

Newport Academy. (n.d.). *Building resilience in children and teens.* Retrieved from https://www.newportacademy.com/resources/well-being/resilience-in-teens/

Office of Population Affairs. (n.d.). *Healthy relationships in adolescence.* Retrieved from https://opa.hhs.gov/adolescent-health/healthy-relationships-adolescence

OpenAI. (2024). *ChatGPT (GPT-4)* [Large language model]. Retrieved August 5, 2024, from OpenAI Platform.

Parent and Teen. (n.d.). *Peer pressure: Strategies to help teens handle it effectively.* Retrieved from https://parentandteen.com/handle-peer-pressure/

Raising Children Network. (n.d.). *Conflict management with pre-teens and teenagers.* Retrieved from https://raisingchildren.net.au/teens/commu nicating-relationships/communicating/conflict-management-with-teens

Raising Children Network. (n.d.). *Getting and giving sexual consent: Talking with teenagers.* Retrieved from https://raisingchildren.net.au/ teens/communicating-relationships/tough-topics/getting-giving-sexual-consent-talking-with-teens

Spark & Stitch Institute. (n.d.). *Teenage dating: Romance and the brain.* Retrieved from https://sparkandstitchinstitute.com/teenage-dating-romance-and-the-brain/

Teen Talk. (2012). *Role plays - Teen Talk.* Retrieved from https://teentalk. ca/wp-content/uploads/2014/05/Communication-Activity_TeenTalk-2012.pdf

Tilly's Life Center. (2022, October 25). *The mental health benefits of journaling for teens.* Retrieved from https://tillyslifecenter.org/2022/10/25/journaling-for-teens-mental-health-resources/

Verywell Family. (n.d.). *How to give your teen constructive criticism.* Retrieved from https://www.verywellfamily.com/how-to-give-your-teen-criticicism-4086439

Verywell Mind. (n.d.). *10 signs of a toxic friend (and how to break up with them).* Retrieved from https://www.verywellmind.com/signs-of-a-toxic-friend-8430982

VirtualSpeech. (n.d.). *Examples of positive and negative body language.* Retrieved from https://virtualspeech.com/blog/examples-positive-and-negative-body-language

Wilde, O. (n.d.). *Be yourself; everyone else is already taken.* Widely attributed.

www.ingramcontent.com/pod-product-compliance
Lightning Source LLC
Chambersburg PA
CBHW011222120626
46545CB00010B/3111